# List of content

List of essay outlines ................................................................... p 2

Advice for students' .................................................................... p 3

Part I: the origins of the Cold War and the early development 1945-53 .. p 5

Student activities 1 ..................................................................... p 25

Part II: 1953-1969 confrontation and détente. ............................. p 41

Student activities 2. .................................................................... p 63

Part III: Détente ......................................................................... p 78

Student activities 3 ..................................................................... p 92

Part IV: the coming of the Second Cold War and the collapse of the USSR p 104

Student activities 4 ..................................................................... p 121

Part V: Germany and China during the Cold War ....................... p 132

Part VI: the nuclear arms race and the major arms agreement ........ p 138

Further reading ........................................................................... p 141

References ................................................................................. p 142

## List of essay outlines:

1. To what extent was the Cold War a result of World War II?
2. "The Cold War was a result of two conflicting ideologies". How far do you agree?
3. "The Cold War was mainly caused by fear and less due to aggression". Do you agree?
4. How is it possible to explain the emergence of the Cold War by referring to events from the period 1945-50?
5. To what extent had the policy of containment been successful in Europe and Asia 1947-50?
6. To what extent was the Korean War a part of the Cold War?
7. How were the Truman Doctrine and the policy of containment implemented in the period 1947-61?
8. Why and with what results did the USSR place missiles in Cuba in 1962?
9. Why has Cuba been an important country in Cold War history?
10. Why was Germany a centre of Cold War problems in the years 1945-61?
11. "The Asian development of the Cold War was far more dangerous than the European development". With reference to events from the period 1945-60, how far do you agree?
12. "It is unjustified to see Khrushchev as a Cold Warrior". Do you agree?
13. Assess the role played by Vietnam in the Cold War.
14. How did the Vietnam War affect the Cold War?
15. How and why was there a period of détente in the 1970s?
16. Why was détente brought to an end in the late 1970s?
17. To what extent did military expenditures lead to the end of the Cold War?
18. To what extent was it external pressure which led to the collapse of the Soviet system?
19. Was Gorbachev responsible for the collapse of the Soviet system?
20. Assess the importance of détente in ending the Cold War
21. What role did Germany play in the Cold War?
22. What role did China play in the Cold War?
23. What were the main events in the arms development 1945-1991?

# Advice for students'.

There are several things you should think about when you read this guide:
**Firstly**, some areas need to be emphasised more than others due to your syllabus and the way in which questions are worded in IB exams. Some areas are central to IB exams, namely: **The Origins of the Cold War, containment and the Truman Doctrine, the Korean War, Germany and the Cold War, the French Indo China War and the Vietnam War, Cuba and the Cold War and the end of the Cold War**. We will cover these in more detail.
**Secondly,** we are preparing you for Cold War questions in the exam. This means that the topics above will be explained in a Cold War context. To give you an example we will show, how the Vietnam War affected and was affected by the Cold War i.e. we are not describing the actual war itself but its implications on the Cold War. We will hopefully provide you with relevant texts or summaries that will complement other sources available.

This brings us to our **third point**. The aim of the guide is to **maximise your performance** in the exam room. Therefore you need to think beyond the actual historical account. You also need to understand the nature of the questions that you will be asked in the exams. This awareness, to which we hope we may be able to contribute, will enable you to focus on the right things when you are reading and preparing for the exam. We will provide you with comments about this, along with essay outlines on central questions. Once you have studied one period, try to outline an answer to an exam question. This is a very important part of your preparation.

We have chosen not to follow the structure of the syllabus in this guide. We want you to understand the topic in depth. Many events that took place can be seen as a response to other events. A chronological account will provide you with a deeper understanding of developments. We have outlined questions which relate to one point in the syllabus in the "essay outline part". This emphasises points mentioned in the syllabus. If we are writing and explaining the period up to the early 60s, there may be a question which refers more specifically to one point in the syllabus, Germany. By reading the chronological account of the Cold War you will be able to understand why many events outside Germany affected the country. Then there will be a question which specifically covers one part of the syllabus: "Why was Germany a centre of Cold War problems in the years 1945-61?"

It is absolutely necessary to have some basic knowledge about how to write or structure an essay. There will be a number of **essay outlines with suggested answer points** included in this guide. We suggest you use the following technique:
- Do your reading
- Answer one of the questions which relates to one Cold War topic.
- Compare your answer with the essay outline.

There are many approaches you can use to answer an essay question. So if your answer does not fully correspond to the outline it is not necessarily wrong. Try to assess and discuss the outline and your answer. We often recommend our candidates to spend some time discussing essay outlines in pairs and ask questions like, "How would you answer this question? You didn't cover point "x" – how come?" This is a highly effective method <u>once</u> you have done some reading.

There are some major types of questions that you need to be able to structure:

### 1. List questions:
Examples:

What were the main reasons for the Cold War?
In what way did the Cold War affect the economic development of Cuba after 1960?

The first question asks you to list all the reasons that you know that led to the Cold War. The second question does the same. Just "list" all possible implications of the Cold War on the Cuban economy. It is also possible to ask "why" a certain event occurred, resulting in a "list-structure".

If the question asks you to **"analyse the reasons for"** an event, it is similar to a list question. What you do additionally is assess each point in the list question more critically, presenting both support and counter arguments to each point.

> **2. "Yes or no questions", "to what extent", "assess the importance", "how far", "discuss" questions.**

These questions require the same type of answer: one part showing "to what extent it was" and a second part showing "to what extent it was not".
Let us give you some examples:

**"The Cold War was a result of World War II*?"* This is called a "yes or no question"** because it can be answered with either a "yes" or a "no" – consequently you must first write a "yes part" showing how the Cold War can be seen as a result of WWII and then a second part, or a "no part", showing that the Cold War resulted from other reasons than just the effects of W.W.II.

**"To what extent was the Cold War a result of W W II*?"*** Is just another way of expressing a "yes or no question" It means that you have to write one part showing how W.W.II led to the Cold War, and a second part showing that the Cold War developed due to events not related to W W II.

**"Assess the importance of W. W. II in the emergence of the Cold War".** The question asks you to show the importance of W.W.II on the Cold War in the first part of the essay. In the second part you should show how factors not related to W. W. II, contributed to the Cold War.

**"How far was World War II responsible for the emergence of the Cold War*?"*** You need to do the same here: show the importance of W.W. II and in the second part show other reasons that had nothing to do with W. W. II.

**"The Cold War was a result of W.W.II" Discuss the validity of this claim concerning the emergence of the Cold War".** Show the importance of W.W.II in the first part of the essay and show all other reasons in the second part of the essay.

> We often advise students to write two lists. One describing "yes" arguments, and one describing "no" arguments. While some teachers may think this is too simplistic, our aim is to help students in preparing each question in the best way possible. It doesn't mean they have to slavishly follow this advice.

> **3. "Compare and contrast" questions.**

**"Compare and contrast the aims and the policies of the two superpowers between 1945-1949."**
The question asks you to show the **similarities** and the **differences** between the two superpowers. You can do this in two ways:
 a) Firstly, explain the aims and the policies of one superpower, and then do the same with the second superpower. After that, and before your conclusion, outline the similarities and the differences.
 b) If the question is extensive, start immediately with the similarities between the superpowers and then show the differences in the second part of the essay. Some years ago there was an exam question which asked "Compare and contrast the reasons for W.W.I and W.W.II". It is clearly impossible to use alternative A here, i.e. first write about the reasons for W.W.I and then continue with the reasons for W.W.II, and finally show the similarities and differences. It is not possible to do this in 45 minutes. The only manageable way is to start immediately with the similarities and then the differences between the two wars. However if you feel you could treat this in the same way as alternative A then keep in mind the time scale. Make your decision before you start to write. B is normally the best alternative.

# Part I: The origins of the Cold War and the early development 1945-53.

(Note: when Churchill talked about an Iron Curtain from Stettin in the Baltic to Trieste in the Adriatic in 1946, he didn't realise that the eastern zone of Germany would be within the Eastern bloc and that Yugoslavia was outside the Eastern bloc after 1948. If you study the map it is possible to find Churchill's Iron Curtain i.e. Stettin to Trieste. This map above shows the Iron Curtain after 1948)

## Overview

As we mentioned in the preface, the early years of the Cold War are of major importance when you study the whole topic. Trying to find an explanation for the Cold War implies that you need to be able to answer the questions:

> 1. What was the Cold War?
> 2. When did it start?
> 3. How would you explain the different ideologies?
> 4. How important were events before and during W.W.II?
> 5. Who was responsible for the Cold War?

Ideologically the USSR and the US represented two fundamentally different systems. There had already been major problems during the war and the alliance was more a result of a necessity to fight a mutual enemy than an expression of genuine understanding. It is clear that the US came out of the war as an economic superpower with access to nuclear weapons, while the USSR was in ruins. As soon as the enemy, or enemies i.e. Germany and Japan were defeated, problems started to arise. Some historians argue that the Cold War started in July 1945, at the **Potsdam Conference**. Others argue that the dropping of the **atomic bomb** in August 1945 was the actual start of the Cold War, as the Americans didn't inform their ally, USSR, about the bomb. Between 1945-48, Stalin violated his promises to allow **free elections in Eastern Europe**. Together with the restart of the Civil War in China, this development alarmed the Americans. In 1947 President Truman announced his **Truman Doctrine,** a commitment initially made for Greece and Turkey, but soon extended globally. It was the most significant change of US foreign policy in the 20$^{th}$ century and isolationism was replaced by a commitment to fight communism globally. It has been seen as the official start of the Cold War. It was followed by the **Marshall Plan,** a US pledge to support the Western democracies economically.

**Germany** was the main trouble spot in Europe. Berlin was located in the Russian controlled Eastern zone i.e. a capitalist island in a communist area. In 1948, Stalin tried to solve this problem by cutting off all land routes from the Western zones. It resulted in a one-year **airlift** with supplies from the West. It was now obvious that it was impossible to unite the different zones. The year after, two independent German states were announced. This year, 1949, also resulted in two major blows to the US: **China**, the most populous state in the world, became a communist state and the Russians exploded their first atomic bomb.

In 1950 North Korea attacked South Korea. After having "lost" Eastern Europe to communism in 1945-48, and watched China became a communist state in 1949, the Americans decided to turn the Cold War into a "hot" war. The Korean War lasted between 1950-53 and it was not until Stalin died in 1953 and Eisenhower replaced Truman, that it was possible to seek new positions. In 1953 both the US and the USSR had hydrogen bombs and a nuclear arms race had begun.

The first part of the Cold War, 1945-53, turned two allies into enemies in a global conflict. The two superpowers had gone from cautious optimism in 1945 to a fierce struggle for world domination.

To be able to answer questions about the origins of the Cold War you need four things:

1. You have to know how W.W.II affected East-West relations.
2. You have to know the main differences in their ideologies.
3. You have to know the main events between 1945-50.
4. You have to know the historiography.

**Two different ideologies.**

**The Cold War can be defined as a state of permanent hostility between two systems and this conflict could never be allowed to erupt into a "hot war" or armed conflict due to the fear of a nuclear war.** This war could be fought by different means i.e. not necessarily armed conflicts. It could be that one "client state" (ally or satellite) was fighting a war against one of the superpowers, as in Korea, but it is worth noticing that there was no major armed confrontation between the USSR and the US between the years 1945-89.

The term "cold war" had first been used in the fourteenth century to describe hostilities between Christians and Muslims. But it was an American journalist, Walter Lippman, who started to use the term to describe the relations between the US and the USSR after 1945. **Karl Marx** wrote in the Communist Manifesto from 1848 that the ruling classes should tremble at the Communist revolution.

Marx

Lenin

**Lenin his disciple, wrote**:
*"Bolshevism can serve as a model of tactics for all" proletarians in the whole world."*[1]

**Adolf Hitler** also realised what the future would bring. In his "Testament" written in April 1945 he wrote:
*"With the defeat of the Reich...there will remain in the world only two great powers capable of confronting each other, the United States and Soviet Russia. The laws of both history and geography will compel these two powers to a trial of strength, either **military** or in the fields of **economics** and **ideology**."*[2]

> You need to be able to discuss the importance of ideology as one reason for the Cold War. You should be able to explain the ideologies of the two superpowers. Let's do that by investigating four vital areas within society:

**Marxism-Leninism versus liberalism and market economy, i.e. the ideologies.**

## A. The economy:

The idea of a **communist society** or Marxism-Leninism is that the state controls the means of production i.e. a rejection of private capitalism and private companies. To achieve an equal society, the state must plan how resources shall be used and how the result of the production shall be distributed. State control of the means of production is a necessary prerequisite in creating an equal and classless society. Common ownership will guarantee both equality and wealth. In Soviet Russia it led to a nationalisation of both land and companies, without compensation to the previous owners. A worker in a capitalist society is exploited by the capitalists. Consequently a true Marxist wants to liberate oppressed workers in other countries. The rejection of private capitalism and a desire to "liberate" oppressed workers in other countries terrified conservative politicians in Western countries. "Let the ruling classes tremble", said Marx.

In a **capitalist society** private ownership and private companies are cornerstones of the society. Competition and a free market produce wealth, and government intervention is normally seen as a negative thing. Even though some state intervention may be acceptable to secure a free market, it is entrepreneurship, trade etc., that will guarantee prosperous economic development. The Americans wanted free trade between states to endorse economic growth and ship products to the consumers. This policy was referred to as an "**open door policy**". From a Russian point of view, this was only a new form of imperialism. By creating economic dependence, the political life of each country would later be controlled. The American demand for "equal rights" was a demand for economic conquest.

## B. Political life.

In the USSR the communist party represented the interests of the working class and the masses so consequently there was no need for other parties. Soviet Russia was a **single party state** and by representing the interest of the masses, it was claimed to be democratic.

In a Western society the existence of a political opposition in a **multi party system**, guarantees a democratic system. The people are offered the opportunity to replace the government in times of election. Freedom of speech, association, the press, and free elections are essential in preserving a true democratic system. A single party system is seen as non-democratic. The USSR however blamed the Western democracies for being non democratic by allowing richer classes to influence political parties and media in the West.

## C Religion.

In a communist society religion was seen a means by which the richer classes could control and oppress the poorer classes. A Russian Marxist was by definition an atheist.
Even though religion and the state are formally separated in the US constitution, it is clear that there is a strong Christian evangelical tradition and that religious groups are of major importance in political life. "Godless communism" scared many Americans during the Cold war.

## D Civil rights.

Both systems claimed that they were democratic and blamed the other side for not respecting democratic rights. Soviet Russia claimed that it exercised the **"dictatorship of the proletariat"** i.e. a transitional stage before a classless society, communism, was achieved. During this "dictatorship" the majority exercised control over the minority. Some restrictions concerning civil rights had to be temporarily imposed. This minority was the old elite and was now prevented from interfering and controlling political life. By restricting freedom of speech for a minority, a more democratic society was established. After this period everyone would realise the benefit of socialism and the final stage, a communist classless society, would be accomplished. The USSR blamed the Western democracies for being non-democratic by allowing richer capitalists to influence the media.
In the US, freedom of speech, the press, assembly and worship are seen as major building blocks in their democratic society and are guaranteed in the constitution. The Americans clearly rejected the Soviet view of a Western society dominated by a few capitalists. In contrast, communist societies controlling the press and imprisoning political opponents were seen as brutal dictatorships.

> Later we shall discuss how different events during the early phase of the Cold War might have affected the other side, like Stalin's behaviour in Eastern Europe and the American Marshall Plan. From an ideological point of view it is possible to understand how each side's policies provoked the other. **It is also clear that the Soviet and the American systems opposed each other in every vital ideological aspect, i.e. the economy, political life, religion and civil rights.**
> Make sure that you can describe the difference between the ideologies – it is very important.

## Tension between the USSR and the US before W.W.II.

It is possible to trace the origins of this conflict to the very foundation of the Bolshevik state in Russia in 1917. The new Bolshevik regime strongly believed that in order to survive it had to stimulate revolutions in other countries, i.e. a **world revolution**. The early development in the Weimar Republic can be seen against this background. The Comintern (the Communist International) was set up to promote this development in 1919. From 1918 to 1921, the new Russian regime had to fight a **civil war** against the White forces, made up of different groups opposing the new regime. The Whites were supported by Western powers fighting in World War I. The Western powers claimed that they wanted to re-open the Eastern front after the Bolshevik regime had signed the Treaty of Brest Litovsk. The Western powers continued the fight against the new regime in Russia, even after the war had ended. It was now clear to the Bolsheviks that capitalists were not prepared to accept a state based on Marxist ideology. After leaving Russia, the intervention was replaced by an economic embargo and it was not until 1933 that the US and the USSR established diplomatic relations. There was no major difference to Stalin between the capitalist states and to him it was only a confirmation of his worst fears when France and Britain did nothing to prevent Hitler's expansion in the mid 1930s. The **Munich agreement** in 1938 forced Stalin to turn to his arch enemy Adolf Hitler, when signing the **Non Aggression Pact** in August 1939. From a Western point of view, Stalin had clearly shown that he was a ruthless dictator by signing a pact with another ruthless dictator, which enabled Hitler to attack Poland.

## In what way did World War II contribute to the Cold War?

The outcome of the war had a major importance for the development of the Cold War. Remember that officially the two superpowers were allies during the war:

1. The war resulted in **two superpowers** with totally opposing ideologies. After W.W.II we start to use the term "superpower" instead of a "great power".
2. One of these superpowers had a **nuclear monopoly**. The atomic age had a profound effect on international relations. See point 9 below.
3. **The USSR had suffered enormously** from W.W.II: 25 million people were killed, 1 700 cities and 70 000 villages were in ruins, 70 % of her industries and 60 % of her transportation facilities were destroyed. It can clearly be questioned if it is correct to describe the USSR as a "superpower" after the war.
4. **The US had experienced a wartime economic boom**. The industrial output of the US grew by 90% between 1940-44.Taking this into consideration, and the fact that the Americans had a **nuclear monopoly**; it can be argued that the Americans have never been as strong as they were just after the war. On the other hand industrialists and politicians were worried that the end of the war would bring and end to this development. International trade and an "Open-door" policy would compensate for the loss of war production.
5. **Germany** did not exist politically and economically when the war ended. There was an enormous **power vacuum** in the centre of Europe which is one major reason for the Cold War. Decisions were made at Yalta and Potsdam in 1945 to divide Germany into "zones of occupation" (see below) and that there should be a Western zone in Berlin, totally surrounded by the Russian zone. This would later create a lot of problems.
6. **The Red Army had liberated and controlled most of Eastern Europe**. How would Stalin use this control? In 1945 he claimed: *"Whoever occupies a territory also imposes on it his own social system. Everyone imposes his own system as far as his army has power to do so. It cannot be otherwise."*[3] In 1944 Stalin and Churchill had concluded the "Percentages Agreement" concerning influence in South-East Europe (the Balkans). The ratios for Britain and the USSR were: Romania: 10:90, Greece 90:10, Bulgaria 25:75, Hungary 25:75, Yugoslavia 50:50. Notice that it didn't involve Poland and Czechoslovakia. Churchill later claimed in his memoirs: "(We) *were only dealing with immediate wartime arrangements.*"[4] Was this the case or did he only try to justify his actions? And what was Stalin's interpretation?
7. During the war, Japan occupied **Korea, China and Indochina** (Vietnam, Laos and Cambodia). In 1943, Churchill and Roosevelt had issued the Cairo Declaration: *"Japan will also be expelled from all other territories which she has taken by violence and greed…Korea **shall become free and independent.**"*[5] This commitment was confirmed by the USSR, Britain and the US at Potsdam. It was stated that *"The terms of the Cairo Declaration shall be carried out."*[6]
Both Korea and Vietnam should be temporarily divided and later unified. Would it work? Would the Civil War in China restart? Like Europe, there was clearly a **"power vacuum" in Asia** after the Japanese surrender.

**Events from the war soured relations:**
8. Even though the US and the USSR had been allies during W.W.II, there were reasons for distrust, not only from a political and ideological point of view. The USSR had signed the **Nazi-Soviet pact** in 1939 enabling Hitler to start the war. The question of a **Second front** in Europe had divided the allies. Stalin wanted help to ease the burden of the Red Army after the German invasion in 1941. It was not until 1944 that the Western powers finally invaded France and opened a real "Second Front" in Europe. Was it a deliberate move to let the USSR bleed to death? Stalin said: "90 Russians died for every American who was killed", (330 000 compared to 25-30 million).
9. The War ended with the Americans dropping an A-bomb on **Hiroshima and Nagasaki.** The USSR had promised the Americans to join them in defeating Japan at Yalta. Now the Americans dropped the bomb without informing her major ally only two days before the Russian attack. Historians have argued that it was the last battle of W.W.II and the first battle of the Cold War.

Finally there were two wartime conferences which were of major importance. Some of the decisions at these conferences have been partly covered above:

## Yalta February 1945.

**1. Poland** was moved 300 km to the West. A compromise was reached over the future government when Stalin promised that some members of the London government (pro-Western) should join the Lublin government (pro-Soviet). "The Declaration of Liberated Europe" was signed by Stalin promising free elections in Eastern Europe.
**2. Japan**: Stalin promised to help the Americans in defeating Japan and to declare war 2-3 months after the war had ended in Europe.
**3. United Nations:** A renewed attempt towards collective security was agreed upon and Molotov would attend the first meeting at San Francisco in April 1945.
**4. Germany:** Should be de-Nazified and was divided into four zones of occupation i.e. an American, Russian, British and French-zone. Berlin was also divided into different zones and the result was a Western zone within the Eastern zone. The establishment of zones of occupation had been decided at a series of conferences and the French zone was added at Yalta. The Berlin solution was probably Stalin's worst mistake because the Berlin problem would later cause major problems to the USSR. The Berlin Wall would later be the symbol of Soviet control of Eastern Europe. Germany should be governed by an Allied Control Council with veto rights for each power. The reparation issue was not solved but handed over to a Reparation Commission.
Yalta is normally considered as a "success." Agreements were made over Germany, Japan, Poland and the United Nations.

"The Big Three" at Yalta

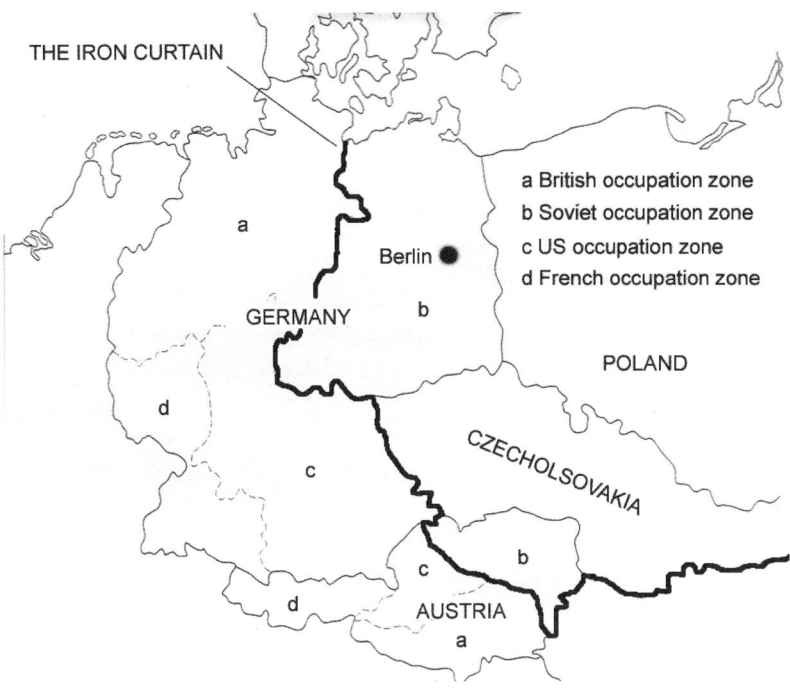

**Potsdam July 1945** (The war had now ended in Europe but Japan did not surrender until August 1945).

**1. Germany**. The zonal division of Germany was finally confirmed in the "Potsdam Protocol on Germany". No final agreement was reached over reparations. Russia demanded some $20 billion from Germany, which was rejected by the Western powers. Russia was left to take what it could from their zone of occupation and to get some reparation from the Western zones.

**2. Eastern Europe:** Western leaders were deeply shocked over developments in Eastern Europe. There were "sharp exchanges" and the West claimed that Stalin didn't follow the spirit of the **Declaration of Liberated Europe.**

**3. Japan:** The Potsdam Proclamation called for Japan's unconditional surrender: *"The alternative for Japan is prompt and utter destruction"*[7], according to the Potsdam Proclamation.

Truman knew at Potsdam that the bomb would work and wanted to end the conflict on his own terms. Stalin was prepared to take part in the defeat of Japan and did not desire a quick Japanese surrender.

**4. Vietnam and Korea:** In Asia, Japan had occupied **Korea, China and Indochina**. In 1943, Churchill and Roosevelt had issued the Cairo Declaration: *"Japan will also be expelled from all other territories which she has taken by violence and greed......**Korea shall become free and independent.**"*[8]
At Potsdam this commitment was confirmed by the USSR, Britain and the US. It was stated that *"The terms of the Cairo Declaration shall be carried out."*[9] Agreements were made to divide the countries temporarily and then unify them later.

Potsdam in normally described as a failure filled with disputes. Some historians even see the Potsdam meeting as the start of the Cold War.

---

We will make a final assessment of the importance of events of World War II on the Cold War later when we have studied the events between 1945-50.
We know from experience that it is difficult to remember and to separate different events from the Yalta and Potsdam conferences. We recommend that candidates remember two words: **PJUG** (Poland, Japan, United Nations, Germany) for Yalta and **GEJV** (Germany, Eastern Europe, Japan, Vietnam/Korea) for Potsdam.

## Historiography.

Before describing developments that took place after the war, we would like to introduce some of the major interpretations concerning responsibility for the Cold War.

**The Orthodox view:** Stalin and the **ideology of Marxism-Leninism** were responsible for the Cold War. To Americans it was in the nature of communist ideology to attempt to spread the ideal of communism. Marxist-Leninism was an expansionist, aggressive force formally claiming that the aim was to "liberate the masses" from capitalism. Throughout his whole career, Stalin had clearly shown that he tolerated no rivals. His policy in Eastern Europe after the war is a very good example. Not only did he violate his promises from Yalta in the **Declaration of Liberated Europe** promising *"free elections of Governments responsive to the will of the people and to facilitate where necessary the holding of such elections"*[10]; he also introduced and imposed a brutal political control of **Eastern Europe**, executing many of his political opponents. These states should have been seen as independent sovereign states, but they were soon referred to as Soviet "satellites". Arthur Schlesinger writes: *"Leninism and totalitarianism created a structure of thought and behaviour which made post-war collaboration between Russia and America.....inherently impossible."*[11]

It is interesting to notice that Stalin's responsibility for the Cold War has survived the opening of Soviet archives in the mid 1980s. John Lewis **Gaddis** writes in **We now Know, rethinking the Cold War**: *I think the "new" history is bringing us back to an old answer: that as long as Stalin was running the Soviet Union a Cold War was unavoidable."*[12]

**The Revisionist view**: emerged from mainly American historians in the late 60s. The US didn't realise how weak the Soviet Union was after WW II and how much stronger the Americans were. Russia had suffered enormously during W.W.II, while the Americans not only experienced **an economic boom**; they also had a **nuclear monopoly**. Stalin realised Russia's weaknesses and his desire to control Eastern Europe was mainly a defensive move to protect the USSR. How did the Americans use their superiority? They issued the **Truman doctrine** giving them a right to intervene everywhere. The US tried to impose its ideals on other people and American values of liberty and free markets should be applied worldwide. After W.W.II the Americans had the military power to enforce their will – and consequently tried to do this. With the Marshall Plan and their economic **"open door policy"** they tried to control countries by economic dependence. Old-fashioned colonialism had never been popular in the US due to the simple fact that the US had once been a British colony. But with this new form of imperialism, where economic dependence would be exploited politically, there was no need for traditional formal political control. It was referred to by the Russians as "dollar-imperialism". William Appelman Williams writes: *"It was the decision of the United States to employ its new and awesome power in keeping with the traditional Open Door Policy which crystallized the cold war...."*[13]

**The Post revisionist view**. With access to new archives a new school of post revisionist historians emerged in the late 1970s. The Cold War was a result of mutual misunderstandings and overreactions due to **fear** from both sides**.** The Americans didn't really understand the USSR's need for security against the West and her need for buffer states and how their strength and "open-door policy" affected the USSR.

The Russians didn't fully realise how their policy in Eastern Europe affected opinions in the West.

It is clear that the development of nuclear weapons and the different ideologies of the two countries resulted in a lot of mutual misunderstandings and fear. Defensive measures by one power were often seen as offensive by the other power. This was met by further measures and a dangerous cycle of action and reaction came into being. The outcome, especially if we take into account the development of nuclear weapons, was less security for both sides. This is called the **security dilemma**. The post-revisionist historians argue that it was more **miscalculations** and fear by both which created the Cold War. Melvyn Leffler writes: *"...The Kremlin was so totalitarian and repressive. US officials intelligently decided to rebuild Western Europe.... These actions were of decisive importance in fuelling the Cold War.... Western Europe required security guarantees, not the extensive armaments that America wanted it to have."*[14]

Finally a few words about **the "Realpolitik" School** with its roots in Bismarck's Germany. According to this school some politicians tend to ignore their ideology when dealing with other states, as long as it is to their benefit. When discussing the Cold war it is clear that "ideology" is a key word. It is therefore useful to be aware of the Realpolitik School which **dismisses the idea of the importance of ideology**. Ideology is only an additional weapon deliberately used by the superpowers to rally the support of the nation. It is a propaganda tool and a mask used to get support while trying to fulfil their state interests. Economic pressure, military power and ideology were means used to achieve an aim. It is clear that both superpowers used ideological arguments to get support from their nations. Could it be that American politicians talked about "Godless communism" when in fact they wanted access to a new and important market? Or did Stalin and the Soviet leaders depict a hostile and dangerous surrounding capitalist world threatening the USSR just to get support for traditional Russian expansion, this time in Europe? Richard Nixon was a well known anti-communist who was prepared to cooperate with both the USSR and China, as long as the US gained from this cooperation. Historians believing in the Realpolitik school would downgrade the importance of ideology in explaining the origins of the Cold War and argue that other reasons were behind this conflict.

Make sure that you can explain the arguments of these four schools.

Franklin D. Roosevelt

**What were the post-war aims of Roosevelt?**

- **The world should be open to free trade i.e. the "Open Door" policy**. To promote this development the Americans stood behind the creation of two important institutions at the Bretton Woods conference in 1944: the World Bank and the International Monetary Fund.
- **To promote peace and international co-operation**. The idea to make a second attempt with **collective security, the United Nations**, was Roosevelt's idea.
- The Americans rejected the idea of **"spheres of influence"** i.e. that one state should indirectly be controlled by an outside power. **National self determination** (the right to decide in which state a population shall belong), **democratic institutions** and civil rights were cherished by the Americans. The British colonial empire had no strong support in the US which would become obvious in 1946, when Churchill made his Iron Curtain Speech. (A revisionist historian would however question this point arguing that the Americans were looking for their own kind of domination. A new form of economic imperialism derived from their economic domination).
- To continue to maintain **relations that were as good as possible with the USSR.**

**Stalin's post-war aims.**

Joseph Stalin                     Propaganda poster, reading: "Beloved Stalin—fortune of the people"

- Stalin realised that the USSR was severely weakened after the war and that **American aid** could be beneficial to the USSR. The Russians had received aid through the "lend-lease" agreement during the war and wanted to continue this co-operation.
- Russian **security**, i.e. controlling states in Eastern Europe which should be seen as a Russian sphere of influence.
- To prevent a **German recovery**. This aim would be clearly visible in the future in Germany.
- To **regain territories** that had been lost after World War I.

Is it possible to trace the origins of the Cold War in these aims? Were they conflicting?

**1946: The disintegration of the wartime alliance.**

Economic hardship in Western Europe after the war and electoral successes of the communist parties in Italy and France deeply worried political leaders in the West. Tension also rose over the development in **Eastern Europe**. Harassment, terror and rigged elections produced communist single party rule in countries like Bulgaria, Romania, Poland and Hungary in 1946-47. It was a clear violation of the Declaration of Liberated Europe. Western leaders saw the development in Eastern Europe as a first step in taking control of the countries in the West. An attempt to put nuclear weapons under UN control, the **Baruch Plan**, was vetoed by the USSR. The plan would not only prevent the Russians from continuing to develop their own nuclear weapons, it would also bring UN inspectors to the USSR. In **China the Civil War** had restarted and south of China, in **Vietnam** a full-scale war between the French and Vietnamese communists and nationalists, Vietminh, started in 1946.

In 1946 we can see signs of a changing attitude in the West that would progressively lead to the introduction of the Truman Doctrine in 1947:

1. In February George **Kennan,** a diplomat at the US Embassy in Moscow, wrote his **Long Telegram.** It was a report written for the State Department and it was widely circulated within US bureaucracy and provided the intellectual basis for the **"doctrine of containment."** A public version of the Long Telegram was published in a famous article in Foreign Affairs in July 1947, called "the X article". Kennan stated that no long-term co-operation was possible with the Soviet regime and that communism must be contained within its present borders. The USSR was aggressive, expansionist and

hostile and described by Kennan as *"World Communism is like malignant parasite which feeds only on diseased tissue."[15]*
Kennan's Long Telegram influenced Washington to a major extent and is a very important background factor behind the policy of "containment" and the Truman Doctrine issued in 1947. It is however important to notice that Kennan himself questioned Truman's emphasis on military containment. In his memoirs he writes that he *"considered containment as primarily political and economic"*, according to Crockatt.[16]

2. In March the British ex-premier **Winston Churchill** gave his **Iron Curtain Speech** at Fulton in the US.
*"From Stettin in the Baltic to Trieste in the Adriatic an iron curtain has descended across the Continent. Behind that line lie all the capitals of the ancient states of Central and Eastern Europe. Warsaw, Berlin, Prague, Vienna, Budapest, Belgrade, Bucharest and Sofia; all these famous cities and the populations around them lie in what I must call the Soviet sphere".*

Winston Churchill

Chiang Kai-shek, Franklin D Roosevelt, and Churchill at the Cairo Conference in 1943 (see the Potsdam conf.)

The speech appealed for a **renewal of the Anglo-American alliance** as a means of deterring Soviet expansionism. Churchill continued his speech:

*"If the population of the **English-speaking Commonwealth be added to that of the United States**, with all that such **cooperation** implies in the air, on the sea, all over the globe, and in science and in industry, and in moral force…. there will be an overwhelming assurance of security."[17]*

Revisionist historians argue that it was now that **Stalin** definitely decided to "satellite" Eastern Europe. He saw it as a major threat to Soviet security and **answered** in a speech:
*"Mr. Churchill begins to set war loose, also by a racial theory, maintaining that only nations speaking the English language are fully valuable nations, called upon to decide the destinies of the entire world."[18]*

Churchill's speech, which must be today described as 'famous', was initially met with suspicion in the US. US opinion was not yet prepared to regard the USSR as an implacable enemy and many Americans suspected that Churchill simply tried to get US assistance to maintain the power of the British Empire worldwide At the time Britain suffered from an economic crisis and problems in India, Greece and Palestine. It is also clear that the speech did have a major impact on US opinion and contributed to the new policy in 1947.

3. In September the **US Secretary of State, Byrnes,** announced in his **Stuttgart Speech** that the US supported a revival of Germany politically and economically. *"The German people…should now be given the primary responsibility for the running of their own affairs."[19]*

It was clear that Germany constituted a major problem to the occupation forces. In May the US had suspended **reparation** deliveries from their zone to the Russians which was seen as a violation of the Potsdam agreement. Both France and the USSR had good reasons to fear a German recovery. **The Allied Control Council**, which had been set up to govern Germany, never worked due to the **veto-power** of each occupational force. In 1946 it was apparent that the US and Britain had realised that a recovery of Europe was dependent on a German recovery. It was against this background that Byrnes made his speech in September. In 1946 Germany was divided into two hostile camps and each side now started to encourage the revival of German political parties. On 1 January 1947, the British and the US zones were merged into one zone, Bizonia. By now it was possible to foresee that there would be two German states in the future. It was something that Stalin had never realised during the war, accepting West Berlin as a capitalist island in the Eastern zone.


**1947 The Truman Doctrine – the official start of the Cold War?**

Harry S Truman

In 1947 the US adopted a policy of **containment**, influenced by George Kennan. The aim was to prevent the spread of communism beyond its present borders i.e. to contain it within its existing borders. The Americans calculated that they were the strongest country in the world both economically and militarily. By adopting a more active role, they would not only be able to prevent a further expansion of communism, they would also strengthen the "free world." Members of the Truman administration, who still believed in some kind of dialogue with the Russians, were eased out of office. One important change was that Byrnes was replaced as Secretary of State (foreign minister) by general **George Marshall**.

The immediate reason for the Truman Doctrine was that in February Britain informed the US that they could no longer support **Greece and Turkey** economically. Britain had traditionally supported allies in the Eastern Mediterranean against Russian expansion. In 1946 there was a civil war in Greece where the government was fighting a communist-led insurgency. Stalin had announced that he wanted a revision of a treaty from 1936 that had put the **Straits of Constantinople** (Istanbul) under Turkish control. He wanted international control of this important waterway and delivered a strong note demanding this in the summer of 1946.

Truman knew that in order to win over a US **Congress** dominated by **Republicans**, his arguments had to be convincing: *"At the present moment in world history nearly every nation must choose between alternative ways of life",* Truman argued. Some historians claim that he exaggerated the threat from communism when he delivered his speech to the Congress. It is clear that it was a historic moment. The US role of **isolationism** was now, definitely, going to be replaced by an **active world role.** This is the most important turning point in US foreign policy in the 20th century. Initially his request for money was only intended for Greece and Turkey but it was soon extended globally and would lead to both Korea and Vietnam. Truman said:

*"One way of life is based upon the will of the majority.... The second way of life is based upon the will of a minority. It relies upon terror and oppression...it must be the policy of the United States to support peoples who are resisting attempted subjugation by armed minorities or by outside pressures."*[20]

"**Outside pressures**" was of course Moscow, even though Stalin had remained neutral in the civil war in Greece. The Congress granted Truman $250 million to Greece and an additional $150 million to Turkey. Using this help for military needs the communist insurgents were eventually defeated. It was clear that the Turkish government was far from democratic but there would be many more examples in the future where it was more important to be anti-communist than democratic. The US also reorganised its administration. In the **National Security Act** (NSC) from 1947, the War and Navy Department were merged into a new Defence Department and the Central Intelligence Agency (**CIA**) was created.

In June of the same year the Secretary of State George Marshall announced his **Marshall Plan**. This massive economic help for European reconstruction was initially offered to most European countries, even the communist states. But it was soon rejected by the USSR and her satellites. From a Russian point of view, this type of new economic imperialism and dependence had to be turned down. Marshall however stated in his speech: *"Our policy is directed not against any country or doctrine, but against hunger, poverty, desperation and chaos."*[21]

The reasons for this "act of humanity" have been widely discussed by historians. There were probably several reasons:

- Marshall had been in Europe in early 1947 and was appalled at the economic and social situation in Europe. **Help** was definitely **needed**.
- **Political reasons: hunger and poverty were a perfect breeding ground for communism**. The French communist party belonged to the coalition government in the country and the Italian communist party was also very strong. There was a risk that some Western democracies would turn to communism. That Western Europe should be "lost to communism" was unacceptable. The Marshall Plan would bind the states in Europe to the US, not just only economically but also politically.
- An economic slump or Western Europe turning to communism would deprive the Americans of one **important economic market**. The US would benefit from a prosperous Europe.

Truman was able to pass the Marshall Plan through Congress in 1948. He was assisted by a communist takeover in Czechoslovakia the same year (see 1948). The effect of the Marshall Plan is normally considered as **successful** and led to massive industrial growth with a GNP growth in Europe of around 15-25% annually. Financial stability returned. Politically the development in 1947 was a **major turning point**. It was now clear that the US would play an active world role and it is hardly surprising that **Stalin now tightened his grip in Eastern Europe**. The successor of Comintern, the international communist organisation, was formed in 1947 and renamed as **Cominform**. The aim was to control and organise communist activities outside the USSR. Non-communists were expelled from the Hungarian government and developments in both Czechoslovakia and Yugoslavia in 1948 are hardly surprising. The Soviet deputy foreign minister Andrei Vyshinsky said in a speech in the UN in September 1947:

*"The so-called Truman Doctrine and the Marshall Plan are particularly glaring examples of the manner in which the principles of the United Nations are violated....It is becoming more and more evident to everyone that the implementation of the Marshall plan will mean placing European countries under the economic and political control of the United States and the direct interference by the latter in the internal affairs of these countries."*[22]

## 1948 - rising tension.

The establishment of communist rule in Eastern Europe followed a general pattern. The Red Army had liberated the countries from Nazi control and immediately introduced a policy of denazification. Communists who had been educated in the USSR and were loyal to Stalin soon took leading positions within their national parties. Left wing parties were pressured by the communists to join them in **"Popular Fronts"** and they soon dominated national provisional governments by controlling key posts such as **Ministers of Justice, Interior** (controlling the police) etc. By controlling the judicial and repressive systems of the state, the communists were able to **rig elections**, i.e. to ensure communist victories. Political opponents were harassed or simply made to disappear. Between September 1947 and February 1948 all non-communists were purged from the governments in Czechoslovakia, Bulgaria, Romania and Hungary.

Once the political system was controlled, a **Sovietization of other aspects of life like economy, culture, land distribution and media could proceed.** Formally these satellites retained their full independence but they were controlled by the USSR. There were two major exceptions in Eastern Europe: Yugoslavia and Czechoslovakia.

There are many examples from Eastern Europe showing this. In Poland the Peasant Party refused to join the Democratic Front which was requested by the communists. The party was subjected to harassment and terror and elections in 1947 were manipulated. The communist controlled "electoral bloc" got more than 90 % support in the elections. In Hungary the leader of the Smallholders party Bela Kovacs, and other representatives from his party, were arrested by Soviet troops in 1947. In Romania the communists and their allies got 372 out of 414 seats in the elections in 1946. The results had been falsified. In Bulgaria the Fatherland Front secured 90 % of the votes at elections in 1945 and used terror and coercion against the political opposition.

> The development in Eastern Europe is of major importance if you want to support the "orthodox view". It was claimed that Stalin violated the Declaration of Liberated Europe. You must be able to give some examples showing this, when explaining the "orthodox school".

**Yugoslavia** had been liberated from Nazi control by Yugoslav partisans under the leadership of Josip Broz **Tito** – and not by the Russian Red Army. After the war Stalin tried to impose his plans for economic development in Yugoslavia, i.e. to concentrate on heavy industry. Tito resisted this policy and took his own initiatives to form a custom union with Bulgaria and Hungary. Stalin could not allow this form of "national communism" and withdrew his economic and military advisers from Yugoslavia. In June 1948 Yugoslavia was expelled from Cominform, the international communist organisation, accused of "bourgeois nationalism". The Eastern bloc now announced an economic blockade and broke off diplomatic relations. **Yugoslavia was now expelled from the Eastern Bloc,** but Tito and his regime had considerable national support. It was also important that they didn't share a border with the USSR. The US offered considerable financial assistance. The outcome of this crisis led to the creation of a **non-aligned**, non-Stalinist, **communist state**. But it also led to a major purge of **"national communists"** in Russian satellite states. The Yugoslav example should not be copied.

**Czechoslovakia** had been liberated from Nazi occupation by the Red Army. But there was much stronger support for communism in Czechoslovakia compared to other satellites due to "the ghost of Munich." The betrayal by the Western democracies in 1938 had not been forgotten. Communists secured 38 % support in free elections in 1946 and joined a coalition with non-communist parties. In 1947 the country suffered from an economic crisis and the communist party feared that this would affect its chances at the elections in 1948. After disputes within the government regarding nationalisation of industries and land reform, non-communist ministers resigned. The Prime Minister formed a new National Front government with only communists and reliable supporters. When elections eventually took place, the communists won 237 of 300 seats in parliament and soon **all other parties were dissolved**. The only country in the Eastern Bloc with a genuine multi party system had now been transformed to a communist single party state.

In the West and in the US this confirmed the view of the "hardliners". The **coup in Czechoslovakia** helped the US government to pass the Marshall Plan through Congress.

**The first real crisis in Europe during the Cold War was about Germany.** In accordance with the policy announced by Byrnes in his Stuttgart Speech in 1946, the Western occupation powers proceeded in their policy of reviving Germany economically and politically. USSR feared and opposed this development. In January 1947 the US and the British zones had been merged into one zone, Bizonia. In the "London recommendations" in June 1948 the US and some other European states recommended that an assembly should convene from the West German Länder (states within the federation) to draft a constitution. **A currency reform in the Western zones was announced in the same month.** Ten old Reichmarks were replaced by one new Deutschmark. A single Western currency required one national economic policy which was again opposed by the USSR. It was an obvious step towards a pro-Western German state, or an attempt to control the economy in the Eastern zone, according to the Russians. On 23 June the Russians cut off all land links to West Berlin. The city was a capitalist island surrounded by the Russian controlled Eastern zone. 2,5 million West Berliners were now cut off from power, coal and food. Western leaders, hypnotised by Russian strength, **feared an attack in the Western zone of Berlin, and even in the rest of Germany**. Berliners were made a symbol of freedom and the Western powers started an **airlift** resulting in 200 000 flights in ten months, which supplied 2,5 million people with food and other necessities until the blockade was called off in May 1949.

Politically the blockade had been a failure for the Russians. They had tried to starve 2,5 million Berliners and this policy made the population in West Berlin firmly anti-communist. The tension during this crisis also triggered an arms race between the US and the USSR. Most importantly the crisis finally led to **two separate German states** and the formation of **NATO in the following year.**

> Some historians have argued that the Berlin Airlift drew the line in Cold War Europe and that the Korean War would do the same in Asia in the early 50s.

**1949 The formation of two Germanies and NATO. China turns to communism.**

A German Parliamentary Council was convened from the Western zones in September 1948. In May the next year it agreed upon a constitution and in August the **Federal Republic of Germany (FDR) was proclaimed**. Elections were held and Konrad Adenauer from the CDU became the first Chancellor. In September the Russians responded by their acceptance to form a separate East German state, The German Democratic Republic (GDR), led by the German Communist Party (SED):

Europe was separated step by step into two major camps and each camp was consolidated according to the logic and nature of the Cold War. According to this logic there had been a genuine fear that the Red Army would conquer West Berlin as a pretext for an invasion of the Western Zones. It was considered that there was no defence in the Western zones that could match the Red Army. Both Britain and France feared the USSR and realised that they needed American support. The French also had good reasons to fear a revival of their old enemy, Germany. An alliance between the Western powers would *"keep the Russians out, the Germans down and the Americans in."*[23] **NATO** was a major commitment to the Americans. It was the first treaty signed with a European state since 1778, when they had signed an alliance with France. The significance of the Truman Doctrine, or the new world role played by the Americans was now obvious. In April 1949, 12 states joined the organisation when it was founded: United States, Canada, Britain, France, Belgium, Netherlands, Luxemburg, Italy, Portugal, Denmark, Norway and Iceland. West Germany was not a formal member but the territory would be protected by the alliance. Greece and Turkey were added in 1951. It was a full military alliance and according to article 5, *"an armed attack against on one or more ... be considered an attack on them all"*[24] and would be met by armed force. A joint NATO command to co-ordinate the defence of the territories was also formed.

This was seen as a major escalation by Stalin and the USSR but he could find comfort in the fact that the Russians exploded their first **atomic bomb** in the same year. Molotov, the Foreign Minister concluded: *"...the imperialist camp has lost thereby one of its most powerful means of blackmailing people."*[25] In China, Mao's communist forces could proclaim the foundation of The Peoples Republic of **China** in October. The most populous state in the world had now turned to communism and to the Americans this new China was another state controlled by Moscow. Truman was accused of the "loss of China".

**1950 – The Cold War turns hot – The Korean War.**

In early 1950 The National Security Council (NSC) delivered a classified report to the Truman administration known as the **NSC-68** report. It stated, *"Soviet efforts are now directed towards the domination of the Eurasian land mass"*[26] and **recommended a massive US build-up of both conventional and nuclear arms**. It can be seen as a response to an expected increase in Russian aggression as a nuclear power and to the "loss" of China. It was not enough to have a dominant economy. The US needed to be militarily superior to meet the challenge of communism. The US should develop a hydrogen bomb. The problem was that this policy would require higher taxes, i.e. it would cause domestic problems for Truman. In June, North Korea suddenly attacked South Korea and this is considered as a turning point in the Cold War. It was assumed that Stalin had ordered Kim to attack and Soviet aggression would follow in other countries, the Domino Theory. The recommendations of NSC-68 were now implemented and US defence spending went from $13 billion in 1950 to $50 billion within a few years. The Russian A-bomb, the "loss" of China and the Korean War provided senator Joseph McCarthy with ammunition for his witch-hunt in the US in the early 50s.

Today we know that it was Kim Il Sun who persuaded Stalin to finally accept the attack. Kim was a communist dictator in the North facing a right wing dictator in the South, Syngman Rhee.

### Why did Kim want to attack the South?
- Kim can be seen as a Korean nationalist who wanted to unite his country which had been **controlled by the Japanese between 1910-45**, and then divided after the war. The Korean War can also be seen as a **civil war** where Kim Il Sun and Syngman Rhee wanted to **unite** their country. There had been constant border disputes between the two countries before the attack.
- **Ideologically** he had reasons for "liberating" the South from capitalism.
- It can be argued that he **didn't expect the US** to support the South. The US Secretary of State, Dean Acheson held a speech in January that defined what should be considered as being within the US "defence perimeter". Neither Korea nor Taiwan were included.
- **Both US and Russian troops had left** Korea but Stalin had provided Kim with arms. In June 1950 alone, the USSR provided the North with 258 tanks, 178 warplanes and 1,600 artillery pieces.[27] Kim had strong reasons to believe in a brief conflict.
- The CIA estimated that there were 600 000 active members in the communist party in the South, or 10 % of the population. They would support the forces from the North.

### Why did Stalin accept the attack?
- Both Kim and perhaps Mao would become **dependent on the USSR**.
- It would expand and strengthen **communism in Asia**. A united communist Korea would also make Russia's border more secure.
- If Stalin had rejected it, **Kim might turn to Mao**.

### Why did the US support the South?
- **The Truman Doctrine, the policy of containment, the NSC-68 report and the Domino Theory**, all indicated that the US must take action. It was a question of credibility and according to Cold War beliefs, aggression from communists was seen as a test of US determination to defend the free world.
- Truman was under **domestic pressure** due to Eastern Europe's loss to communism between 1945-48, the "loss" of China and the Russian A-bomb in 1949.
- The Cold War had clearly turned more global and **Asia** was now a trouble spot with Mao in China, problems in Korea and the French being embroiled in a full scale war against communist guerrillas in **Vietnam.** Truman said: *"If we stand up to them like we did in Greece three years ago, they won't take any next steps."*[28]

### Why did China support North Korea?
- Mao and Kim had fought together in the Chinese civil war. It was a way of paying Kim back.
- Mao felt threatened when the UN forces, dominated by Americans, were close to the Chinese border,
- Mao clearly wanted to play the role of international communist leader, which would be clearer later,

**The course of the War.** (Note. Make sure you put questions about the Korean War in a Cold War perspective. You are not expected to write an essay about the war but more to discuss it in the context of the Cold War. In topic I, Paper II, however, you may get questions purely about the war).

- The **Cairo agreement** from 1943, stipulated that Korea should regain her independence after the Japanese surrender. This was confirmed at **Potsdam** in July 1945.
- The country was divided along the 38$^{th}$ parallel and the USSR controlled the North while the Americans established control of the South. Soon Kim Il Sun established a Soviet model in the North and Syngman Rhee, a right-wing nationalist established control in the South.

- In 1948 there were elections for a National Assembly but only in the South, where Syngman Rhee was elected president. The same year **two separate Korean states were established**. The division was deeply resented by both sides and the population wanted a unified Korea.
- In late 1948, Soviet troops left the North and in early 1949, American troops left the South.
- **In June 1950, troops from the North suddenly crossed the 38th parallel.**
- In June the UN Security Council took a decision for military action against North Korea. It was decided that South Korea should be re-established i.e. the North should not be conquered. It was possible to pass the resolution without a Russian veto because they were **boycotting** the UN as Red China was not accepted as a representative of China by the **UN**. Taiwan represented China. The Korean War was technically a UN operation and 16 countries participated but it was mainly an American operation with 260,000 America troops compared to 35,000 men from other nations. These troops and the South Korean army were placed under US General Douglas MacArthur who was accountable to President Truman.
- In September the North had conquered the whole of South Korea except for the southeast corner.
- In the same month, MacArthur launched a daring counter-attack from the sea just south of the 38th parallel at **Inchon** — behind the enemy lines — in an attempt to cut off troops from the north.
- Soon the South was recaptured and Truman decided to cross the 38th parallel to capture the North, to roll back the communists. If this had succeeded it would be the first area to be "liberated" from communist control.
- In November, 300 000 **Chinese "volunteers" crossed the Yalu river**, the border between Korea and China, and the Korean War had reached a critical point. In December, UN forces lost 11 000 men in two days and in one of these two days, the Americans lost 3 000 soldiers. Chinese casualties were far higher.
- The Chinese forces soon pushed the UN forces across the 38th parallel again and in 1951 a stalemate was established around the 38th parallel.
- Truman now decided **to "limit"** his war aims, not to conquer the North. This was deeply resented by MacArthur who wanted to widen the conflict and he publicly criticised the president and called his "limited" strategy a form of appeasement. MacArthur wanted to attack China and use soldiers from Taiwan against them. He also issued an unauthorised nuclear threat on China. In April 1950 Truman **dismissed MacArthur** who returned to the US, seen as a hero by many.
- Peace talks began in July 1951 but the war dragged on for another two years around the 38th parallel.
- An **armistice** was not signed until **1953,** when Stalin had died and Eisenhower had succeeded Truman.

## Consequences of the war.

There are many different estimates Korean War victims.

## To South and North Korea.

- **415 000 South Koreans** were killed and **500 000 in the North** (2/3 of the population lived in the South)
- 5 million Korans were homeless, and most of the infrastructure and industries were destroyed. To Korea it was a **"total war".**
- Politically the country remained **divided** and Kim imposed a Soviet style system in the North. In the South, Syngman Rhee established a right wing dictatorship.
- The hostilities between the two Koreas resulted in both countries using vast resources to arm themselves in the future. Resources which could have been used for other purposes.

### To China

- The US made a pledge to defend Taiwan. The fact that China had entered the war, fighting UN/US troops, created hostilities between the two countries that were not resolved until the 1970s. It **isolated China diplomatically** for years. US commitments in Asia after the war also threatened the security of China (see effects to the US)
- It tied China to the USSR. In 1950 a Sino-Soviet Friendship Treaty was signed.
- **China lost around 360 000 soldiers.** (difficult to estimate)

### To the USSR.

- There were now two communist states in Asia, North Korea and China, closely **tied to the USSR.**
- The most important consequence was that the war led to a far-reaching **military build-up** from both sides. In 1953 the USSR had built their first hydrogen bomb. It has been argued by many that the Russians could not bear the cost of this in the long-term. The Korean War can be seen as a major starting point of a militarization of the Cold War which resulted in a larger proportion of USSR's GNP being used for military expenditure.
- The US committed itself even more to the defence of Germany and Western Europe. This would lead to further commitments by the USSR. When Germany was made a full member of NATO in 1955. The USSR formed the Warsaw pact. It was all a greater and more costly escalation.

### To the US

- **33 000 men were killed.**
- It deeply affected public opinion in the US. It is no coincidence that Senator Joseph McCarthy started his witch-hunt for communists in the US during these years.
- The war was an important reason for the election of a Republican as US president after some 20 years. **Eisenhower and his Secretary of State, John Foster Dulles, rejected containment and fighting "limited wars".** They introduced a policy of possible **"massive retaliation"** -the use of nuclear arms and **"roll back"** - a policy of "liberating" communist controlled areas.
- As mentioned before, the **NSC-68 report was implemented** and a substantial increase in military expenditure took place. US expenditure rose from $13 billion to $50 billion per year during the war. It never dropped below $ 40 billions for the rest of the century. NATO was strengthened economically. Decisions were made to re-arm West Germany and let her contribute with troops, to become a full member. A peace treaty was concluded with Japan in 1951 and the country became the key in the US system of alliances in Asia. In 1954 the Americans created the SEATO (the South East Treaty Organisation) made up by the US, France, Britain, Australia, New Zealand, the Philippines, Thailand and Pakistan, in an attempt to fight communism in Asia.
- The US started supporting the French in their war in **Vietnam**. But it was not total support. When the French withdrew from the war in 1954, the Americans were bearing 70% of the cost of the French Indo-China war. But it was the Korean lesson that made Eisenhower introduce his New Look, a. reluctance to fight limited wars in the Third World. Korea affected both Eisenhower and Kennedy in their Vietnam policy and their rejection of sending combat troops.
- The US committed itself to protecting **Taiwan** from an attack by Red China.

**To the UN**

- The UN had shown that it could take action. One of the major reasons for the failure of the League of Nations had been the inability to take action against Japanese aggression in the same area, **Manchuria,** in 1931.
- It was partly seen as a "tool of capitalism" within the communist camp, which weakened its authority.

**What were the consequences in general?**

It is clear that the Korean War had a major impact on the Cold War. What had been declared or indicated in the Truman Doctrine from 1947 had now been implemented. It marks a point where a major escalation took place. The Cold War had been made a "hot war" which was fought by "client states." It is probably correct to conclude that the Chinese entry into the Korean War was one of the most critical moments of the Cold War. It has been argued that the Berlin Blockade "drew the line" in Europe in that it resulted in two German states and the formation of NATO. **The Korean War had the same importance in Asia and led to major commitments from both sides, in Korea, to Japan, Taiwan, China and Vietnam.**

An interesting fact is that many Soviet pilots secretly fought in the war and that many were killed. This was unofficial but it is worth noting that there was also direct armed confrontation between US and Soviet troops during this war.

# Student activities 1.

We have outlined the most important part of the Cold War from the examiners' point of view. This can be concluded by studying how questions are set in exams. Questions about how the Cold War started, The Truman Doctrine, containment and the Korean War are frequent in IB exams. The text provided in this guide may be used as a summary. Your textbook provides a real in-depth study. What is very important is to use this knowledge to structure your essay answer. The questions about the origins of the Cold War do not require an ability to write one full essay about the Truman Doctrine or any other event from the period. You need to use events from the period 1945-50 to answer such a question and to form an argument. So if we should simplify what we have done so far, you are expected to know:

The consequences of **W.W. II** including the Yalta and Potsdam conferences.
The **ideologies** and be able to explain them.
The main interpretations i.e. **historiography**
**1946**
Kennan's Long Telegram
Churchill's Iron Curtain Speech
Byrnes's Stuttgart Speech
The development in Eastern Europe 1945-48
**1947**
The Truman Doctrine and the policy of containment
The Marshall Plan
**1948**
Yugoslavia
The coup in Czechoslovakia
The Berlin Airlift
**1949**
The establishment of two separate German states
NATO
The Russian A-bomb
China turns to communism
**1950-53**
the NSC-68 report
Why the Korean War started

This brings us to the question how or why did the Cold War start? It brings us to an important issue, namely when did it start? Officially there is no formal starting point, even if many historians refer to the Truman Doctrine. We have earlier defined the Cold War as a state of permanent hostile relations between the two camps, which could not be allowed to become "hot" due to the existence of nuclear weapons. It has been argued that:

- The Cold War can be traced back to the Russian Civil War in 1918-21 when the White forces were supported by the Western powers.
- Did it start at the Potsdam conference? There were heated arguments over developments in Eastern Europe. No agreement was made over reparations and Truman, who was informed about the existence of the Hydrogen Bomb during the conference, did not properly inform Stalin, only the British.
- Was it the dropping of the bomb on the 6th of August 1945 that started the Cold War? The USSR meant to attack Japan on the 8th but was not informed by the Americans that they were going to use the bomb. "It was the last battle of. W.W. II but the first battle of the Cold War". The use of the bomb and post-war discussions about how to share nuclear technology deeply affected Stalin.

- How much attention should be paid to the Iron Curtain speech? After all, Churchill was an ex-leader when he made the speech and it was met with suspicion by many Americans. On the other hand, it had a major impact on US opinion and on Stalin. Some historians have argued that Stalin tightened his grip on Eastern Europe after the speech, which deeply affected the West.
- With the Truman Doctrine in 1947 the US officially declared a new role to meet what they perceived as the challenge of communism. The Marshall Plan was seen as "dollar imperialism".

---

- The Cold War was not a "war" in the real sense. Don't use it as an example of a "war" in an essay.
- Without a formal start of this "war" you can only propose and discuss the importance of some starting points like those mentioned above. It is possible to argue that events after 1947 were effects of the Cold War more than causes of the Cold War

---

**Before answering some essay questions, answer the following questions:**

1. In what way did the events of W W II contribute to the Cold War (don't include Yalta and Potsdam)?

2. What was decided at the Yalta and Potsdam meetings?

3. Describe Marxism Leninism and liberalism/market economy.

4. What happened in Eastern Europe between 1945-48 and what was decided at Yalta, which made this development unacceptable to the US? This is important if you want to discuss the development in Eastern Europe.

5. What early sign of a changing attitude from the Western powers could we see in 1946?

6. Why are the Truman Doctrine and the Marshall Aid programme so important?

7. What was the Berlin airlift and what did it lead to?

8. In what way was 1949 a year which brought trouble to the US?

9. Why did the Korean War start?

10. What were the effects of the war?

11. When do you think the Cold War started?

_____
_____
_____
_____

**We shall now outline some typical exam questions on the origins of the Cold War:**

1. To what extent was the Cold War a result of World War II?
2. "The Cold War was a result of two conflicting ideologies". How far do you agree?
3. "The Cold War was mainly caused by fear and less due to aggression". Do you agree?
4. How is it possible to explain the emergence of the Cold War by referring to events from the period 1945-50?
5. To what extent had the policy of containment been successful in Europe and Asia 1947-50?
6. To what extent was the Korean War a part of the Cold War?

**We will provide you with some outlines with suggested answer points. There is normally never a "final" answer to such a question and we think it might be useful to do the following:**

1. Study the question. What does it require? What kind of question is it?
2. Write down your suggested answer points (use the essay plan templates).
3. Study our model answer and compare it with your own. It may be that you have used another approach that is just as relevant. The important thing is to assess and compare the answers.

We think it wise to explain the Cold War from the perspective of the different schools of interpretation. Try to avoid a narrative account where you are simply listing different events in chronological order – use the different schools when explaining the origins of the Cold War. But you must **avoid a historographic "trap"** i.e. you must support each school of thought thoroughly by referring to different events.

| Essay Title: **1. To what extent was the Cold War a result of World War II?** |
|---|
| Introductory points: |
| 1st main part: |
| 2nd main part: |
| Conclusion: |

1. **To what extent was the Cold War a result of World War II?** *(You need to write one part where you show that the Cold War was a consequence of. W.W.II and a second part where you demonstrate that it was a result of other things that had nothing to do with the war)*

**Yes it was a result of the war** (elaborate on the following points):

- The war resulted in two victorious superpowers with totally different ideologies.
- One had a nuclear monopoly and had used the bomb without informing her ally.
- The USSR had suffered enormously from the war while the US emerged stronger than ever. The question of a 'second front' during the war had soured relations.
- The Red Army controlled Eastern Europe, which would have a major significance in post-war Europe.
- Germany did not exist politically and militarily. There was a power vacuum in the heart of Europe. Decisions during the war had resulted in Germany being divided into zones of occupation, Berlin was to have a western zone and there should be a ruling Allied Control Council with veto rights assigned to each occupying power.
- In Asia, Japan had surrendered and control had to be re-established in Korea, China and Indochina.

**No, the Cold War was not a result of the war** *(we are now facing a problem which is difficult to deal with: How shall we discuss post-war history from the perspective of there never having been a W.W.II? It is possible to discuss the following points:)*

- Tension had already surfaced during the Russian Civil War 1918-21 and it took years until the Americans recognised the USSR. Their relations had always been hostile, which was expected.
- Write about how fundamentally different these two systems were from and ideological point of view. It is likely that there would have been tension between these two systems even without the war. Neither believed in a peaceful co-existence. **This is the most important point in part two.**
- You could put yourself in the shoes of an orthodox historian by arguing that a Marxist Leninist system would challenge the free world even without W.W.II. This was inevitable due to the USSR's wish to "liberate" oppressed workers in capitalist countries. Lenin had argued that clashes between the Soviet republic and bourgeois states were inevitable.
- You can use arguments from a revisionist historian. The Open Door policy aimed at dominating other countries economically and this kind of "dollar imperialism" cannot be purely seen as a result of the war and it would of course provoke the USSR.
- To post revisionist historians, "fear" is one key explanation of the Cold War and one reason for this fear was of course nuclear weapons. The construction of nuclear weapons had started before the war and it cannot be argued that nuclear weapons were a result of W.W.II. It is clear that the existence of nuclear weapons in the future would cause tension and this cannot be seen as a W.W.II phenomenon.

**Conclusion**: Cold War questions dealing with responsibility and guilt are clearly controversial and it is not a coincidence that historians are so divided over the issue. In this question however, we think it is possible to conclude that there would be some "cold war problems" even without W.W.II. The war created some problems but these two systems were so fundamentally different that problems would have occurred in some form even without the war. Lenin was correct in his prophecy. But this assumption is of course not a historical fact.

| Essay Title: **2. "The Cold War was a result of two conflicting ideologies". How far do you agree?** |
|---|
| Introductory points: |
| 1st main part: |
| 2nd main part: |
| Conclusion: |

## 2. "The Cold War was a result of two conflicting ideologies". How far do you agree?

*(You have to define and show the importance of their ideologies in the first part of the essay and argue that the problems were not due to ideological difference, in the second part)*

**Yes, ideology was important:**

- **Explain Marxism Leninism** ( the economy, political life, religion and civil rights ) and its desire to expand into other countries. Religion was seen as the "opium of the masses". What a communist perceived as the "dictatorship of the proletariat" was seen by Western observers as a ruthless and totalitarian form of government.
- **Explain capitalism, market economy** ( the economy, political life, religion and civil rights ) **and the "open door policy"** and its desire to expand into other markets.
- **Use examples** illustrating how each side perceived the "other side". For example: what the Americans thought about Russian policy in **Eastern Europe** and in **Asia**. They were horrified over the fact that political opposition was harassed, land and industries had been nationalised without compensation, etc. You can write a lot here. What did the USSR think about the **Marshall Plan** and the **Truman Doctrine**? Why was it so important to revive Germany? Show how they were coloured by their ideologies.

**No, it was not an ideological conflict:**

- Explain the "Realpolitik school", which claims that powers may act out of reasons other than ideology but use ideology to disguise their real intentions or simply as a means of getting support.
- Even if ideology was important, some historians emphasise the importance of W. W. II. The differences of the ideologies existed before 1939, but why did relations collapse after the war? The war created a unique situation where these two superpowers achieved world domination and powers like Germany and Japan were totally destroyed. This situation led to a contest for power globally.
- It is interesting to notice that the Americans were prepared to support non-democratic regimes like Tito in Yugoslavia, Syngman Rhee in Korea, Batista in Cuba and Diem in Vietnam, whose most important qualifications were that they opposed Moscow. Tito was a communist.
- Stalin's expansion into Eastern Europe deeply worried the Western powers. But had this expansion anything to do with communist ideology or was it caused by security reasons or a traditional Russian desire to dominate surrounding countries?

**Conclusion:** It is difficult to totally ignore the importance of ideology during the Cold War. But it is also possible to argue that the results of the war in combination with the ideologies played a role. It can also be argued that ideology was of no importance to a politician like Stalin, thereby supporting the Realpolitik school.

| Essay Title: **3. "The Cold War was mainly caused by fear and less by aggression". Do you agree?** |
|---|
| Introductory points: |
| 1st main part: |
| 2nd main part: |
| Conclusion: |

**3. "The Cold War was mainly caused by fear and less by aggression". Do you agree?** *(In the first part you try to show how fear played an important role. It is a key word in the post revisionist school. In the second part you focus on other reasons, such as aggression.*

**Yes, "fear" was important:**

- The most important point, discussing "fear", is probably to discuss the importance of nuclear weapons. It led to an arms race that resulted in less security for both sides. Explain the "Security dilemma".
- It has been argued that Stalin's policies in Eastern Europe and his need for buffer states were mainly defensive. He *feared* another attack against the USSR through Eastern Europe. His policies in Eastern Europe deeply affected the US. These are arguments used by revisionist historians.
- It has also been argued that the USSR *feared* "dollar imperialism" and consequently had to protect themselves from this new form of imperialism. Economically the US was far stronger than the USSR.
- *Fear* is also a keyword if you want to understand the Truman Doctrine. If communism was not opposed there could be a domino reaction where countries would fall to communism. After the war, Eastern Europe had been "lost" to communism and there were communist advances in Asia: in China, Korea and Indochina. There are many examples to use where "fear" can be found.

**There were clear signs of aggression**

- Put yourself in the shoes of an orthodox historian. Explain the nature of Marxism Leninism and explain Stalin's policies in Eastern Europe, Comintern, the coup in Czechoslovakia, the Berlin airlift and problems all over Asia. Some of them resulted in armed conflicts. It can be seen as communist aggression controlled by Moscow.
- A revisionist historian would be able to describe US policies and beliefs as "aggressive". The US was without doubt the strongest state after the war and had dropped an A-bomb. How did they use this strength? They issued the Truman Doctrine giving themselves the right to intervene anywhere, and the Marshall Plan was an attempt to control weaker states economically and later politically. Again it is possible to give examples from Greece, Taiwan, Korean, Vietnam, etc where this aggression was shown.

**Conclusion**: We support a combination, of fear and aggression. We would, however, not go as far as to say that the Cold War was mainly caused by misunderstandings. Support your argument.

| Essay Title: **4. How is it possible to explain the emergence of the Cold War by referring to events from the period 1945-50?** |
|---|
| Introductory points: |

**4. How is it possible to explain the emergence of the Cold War by referring to events from the period 1945-50?** *(This can be approached in several ways. It is a list question and it is possible to go through the question by writing a chronological account. There is a risk that this will become a narrative account which will not score well. We recommend you use the different schools of interpretation again. It will enable you to write a more analytical essay. **It is however very important to support each school by referring to different events**).*

- Describe the "**orthodox view**" and explain Marxism-Leninism from an ideological point of view. Use examples from the period that will strengthen your argument. Possible points to cover: the **Russian policy in Eastern Europe versus commitments made at Yalta**, the policy in Germany where an economic unity was blocked, the **Berlin airlift, the coup in Czechoslovakia**, Comintern and developments in **China, Korea and Vietnam**.
- A **revisionist historian** would describe this period by explaining how strong the Americans actually were after the war, both economically and militarily. This strength was used to achieve world domination. It is possible to strengthen this view by referring to the dropping of the **a-bomb**, policies in Germany, the **Truman doctrine** leading to support for Greece and Turkey; and perhaps most importantly, the **Marshall Plan** providing for "**dollar imperialism**" and an "Open Door policy". US policies in Asia, such as in Korea, and support for the French in Indochina are also possible points to use. The US also misinterpreted Stalin's foreign policy. They thought that his driving force was an expansionist communist ideology and not national security.
- A **post revisionist historian** would describe the emergence of the Cold War as a result of mutual misunderstandings and fear. The Americans didn't understand that Stalin's aims in Eastern Europe were mainly defensive and that he genuinely feared US military and economic strength. Instead they issued the Truman doctrine aiming at world domination. Stalin was probably not fully aware of how his brutal policies in the satellites affected politicians in the West. It is also clear that with so fundamentally different systems combined with the development of weapons of mass destruction, a lot of fear and misunderstandings were inevitable. Both sides must bear responsibility.

**Conclusion**: summarise your main points and emphasise what you think is important. But notice that the question doesn't explicitly ask you to make your own 'final judgement'.

| Essay Title: **5. To what extent had the policy of containment been successful in Europe and Asia between 1947-50?** |
|---|
| Introductory points: |
| 1st main part: |
| 2nd main part: |
| Conclusion: |

## 5. To what extent had the policy of containment been successful in Europe and Asia between 1947-50? *(Write one part of the essay claiming that it had been successful and a second part showing failures. Note that you must explain the term containment at the beginning of the essay)*

It is always important to define difficult words in the question. "Containment" needs to be defined. **Containment** was the US policy that was adopted by President Truman in his Truman Doctrine in 1947 by which the US attempted **to prevent further Soviet or communist expansion** beyond territories occupied in 1945. No long-term co-operation with the USSR was possible and George Kennan provided the intellectual basis in his Long Telegram from 1946. By supporting the "free world" economically through the Marshall Plan in Europe and economic aid to Japan, the expansion of communism would be prevented.

**Successes:**

- The Marshall Plan led to a substantial economic recovery in Western Europe and it is believable that conditions which bred left wing support were receding as a result of this. The communist parties in both Italy and France lost some of their substantial support in elections in the late 1940s.
- This was probably most obvious in the western part of Germany, which went through a remarkable economic recovery. Germany became a democratic and economically stable country bordering the Eastern Bloc. A pro-western Germany was without any doubt essential for the survival of Western Europe as a part of the "West". The conservative Christian Democrats and Konrad Adenauer were victorious in free elections.
- The Berlin airlift must be described as a "victory". The Americans had been able to support 2,5 million Germans and this support had turned the population pro-American.
- The support for Greece and Turkey enabled these two countries to remain within the Western camp. (Both joined NATO in 1951). The communists had been defeated in the civil war in Greece.
- The building up of a strong Western military alliance, NATO, under American leadership, strengthened the West.
- In the late 40s the Americans successfully started to build up Japan as an ally in Asia and a bulwark against communism.

**Failures:**

- The US build up of Western Europe was a threat from Stalin's point of view, and he strengthened his control of the satellites. The Czech coup in 1948 and a purge against "national communists" can partly be seen as a response to the build up in Western Europe and these counter actions were not "successful" from an American point of view.
- The "loss" of China was a major failure. The most populous state in the world turned to communism and signed a Sino-Soviet Friendship Treaty in 1950. The nationalists in China had received economic aid after 1945, yet they lost the Civil War.
- In 1950 the Korean War started. Even if it was too early to assess the final outcome of this conflict in 1950, it was clear that the Americans were facing an expansionist enemy. At the end of 1950 Red China also attacked the UN forces in Korea.
- In Vietnam the French were fighting a difficult war against communist guerrillas who were not easily defeated. The US had now started siding with an unpopular colonial ruler and feared a domino reaction throughout South East Asia.

**Conclusion:** Summarise the successes and the failures. It is possible to conclude that containment had been more successful in Europe than in Asia.

| Essay Title: **6. To what extent was the Korean War a part of the Cold War?** |
|---|
| Introductory points: |
| 1st main part: |
| 2nd main part: |
| Conclusion: |

**6. To what extent was the Korean War a part of the Cold War?** *(Demonstrate to what extent it was a Cold war conflict and to what extent it was not. It means you have to show both how the Cold War affected the war but also how the Korean War influenced the Cold War).*

**The Korean War was not a Cold War conflict:** *(it is perhaps an unorthodox way of answering the question by starting with the "no" part, but there are fewer "no" arguments compared to the "yes-points", so let's start with the smaller part)*

- Two independent states had been set up in 1948 and both were ruled by non-democratic **nationalist leaders, Kim Il Sun and Syngman Rhee**. Both wanted to unify the country, by force if necessary. Both claimed authority over the whole country. The division of the country was deeply resented by the population.
- **There were ongoing border disputes both in 1948 and 1949, and several thousand soldiers were killed**. There was growing opposition to Rhee's rule and communist guerrillas were fighting the regime in the South. It was more the will to unite the country that made Kim ask Stalin for support. There is one school of historians who argue that the origins of the conflict can mainly be found in this **national question,** and less in the Cold War i.e. it was more like a Civil War in the beginning.
- It can be argued that the there were other reasons than Korean reasons that started the conflict (see below). The relations within the communist camp may have had some importance. It might be that Stalin wanted both North Korea and China to be involved in the war because it would tie them to the USSR. It can be seen as an "internal" communist reason.

**The Korean War was a Cold War conflict** *(notice that the question doesn't explicitly ask for the origins of the conflict. So it is possible to write about the origins and implications from a Cold War perspective).*

- **The Truman Doctrine, the policy of containment and the NSC-68** report all indicated that the US must take action. Truman was also under pressure due to the "loss" of China and the Russian A-bomb. The Domino theory also played an important role.. The Cold War, it must be argued, pushed the Americans into entering the conflict. The war had far-reaching consequences for US policies by increased support to Japan, Taiwan, the French in Vietnam, Europe and the creation of SEATO. It also led to the rise in US military expenditure from $13 billion to $50 billion per year, in other words an implementation of the NSC-68 report. **The consequences show how this conflict can be seen as a part of the Cold War**.
- The reason for the UN acting against the North was a Soviet boycott as Red China was not accepted in the UN.
- The prospect of a capitalist US-led Korea, was unacceptable to China and it led to their **involvement**. The consequences of diplomatic **isolation** for years and US containment policies in Asia, especially regarding Taiwan, show how the conflict can be related to the Cold War.
- In **Europe** the conflict led to NATO being strengthened.
- To **Stalin** a communist expansion would **strengthen the communist camp** and engulf the Americans in a major conflict if they decided to support the south. It would open up possibilities in other areas. This was probably one reason for Stalin finally supporting Kim. The Korean War led to increased tension and a militarization of the Cold War. The **Red Army** doubled in size between 1948-53 to more than 5 million men. One reason for this was the tension that was created by the Korean War.

**Conclusion:** there may have been other reasons behind the conflict but the Korean War was definitely a part of the Cold War both in its origins and consequences.

# Part II: 1953-1969 confrontation and détente.

### Overview

The second period of the Cold War is very much influenced by the **death of Stalin** and the rise to power of Nikita **Khrushchev**. If Stalin had been more of a cautious planner, Khrushchev was much more **adventurous and difficult to predict**. Officially he announced a new policy of **peaceful co-existence** with the capitalist west and started a de-Stalinisation process. But he soon involved the Red Army in crushing the Hungarian uprising in 1956 and issued a Berlin ultimatum in 1958. Most fatal of all, he placed nuclear missiles on **Cuba**. While Stalin had tried to extend Soviet influence in neighbouring countries, Khrushchev intervened in areas like the Middle East and Central America.

The new US administration with President **Eisenhower and the Secretary of State, John Foster Dulles** were both fierce anti-communists and publicly announced in their new foreign policy, known as the **New Look**, plans of **"massive retaliation", "brinkmanship", "roll-back" of communism**, and the necessity of **nuclear superiority.** But the practical outcome was that no real adventurous moves were taken: no support was given to the Hungarians and there was no major escalation in Vietnam.

The **nuclear arms race** escalated and even a space competition started during these years with costs that, with the benefit of hindsight, the Russians couldn't bear. There were also several attempts to establish a dialogue and the 50s witnessed the first summits during the Cold War between the leaders of the super-powers. In 1961 the **Berlin Wall** was erected and the year after witnessed a very dangerous conflict over Cuba, **the missile crisis**. This crisis was one of many reasons for the Sino-Soviet split in the early 60s. The outcome of the missile crisis led to a new period of relaxation and attempts to co-operate which were interrupted by two major conflicts: President Johnson's **escalation of the Vietnam war** and the **invasion of Czechoslovakia** by the Warsaw pact in August 1968.

So the period of 1953-1969 can best be described as a period of <u>both</u> confrontation and détente.

**Time for détente (lessening of tension)? The new Russian leadership after Stalin.**

**Malenkov**

**Khrushchev**

When Stalin died in 1953 there was no clear successor and a collective leadership emerged with Malenkov and Khrushchev as the most prominent leaders. In 1955 Malenkov was ousted by his rival Khrushchev. The new leadership opened up for new opportunities in the Cold War during the years 1953-56:
- An armistice was finally signed in **Korea** in 1953.
- In 1954 a peace conference was arranged at **Geneva** to deal with the **Indo-China war**, under the chairmanship of the USSR and Britain.
- In 1955 there was a Great power summit in Geneva between the USSR, the US, Britain and France. The leaders met for the first time since Potsdam 1945. The new and positive atmosphere was referred to as **"the spirit of Geneva"**.

- In 1955 the occupational forces of **Austria** decided to end the occupation and re-establish full independence of the country. This had not been possible in countries like Germany and Korea. Soviet troops were also withdrawn from Finland.
- Khrushchev started to **reduce the size of the Red Army** unilaterally (without the other side doing it).
- Khrushchev went to **Yugoslavia** in 1955 to heal the rift between the two states and to show that the USSR could accept the existence of a communist regime not totally controlled by Moscow, a clear break with Stalin's policies
- In February 1956 Khrushchev gave a dramatic and important speech at a secret session of the 20$^{th}$ Party Congress i.e. the "**Secret Speech**" in an attempt to promote "de-Stalinisation" and liberalisation. It had far reaching consequences as it started a de-Stalinisation process in the USSR. It can partly be seen as a **domestic political struggle** against old Stalinists like Molotov, but it had international implications as well. In **China**, Mao regarded the attack on Stalin's terror and the cult of personality as an indirect attack on his rule. Khrushchev also announced that there could be **"national roads to socialism"** i.e. an acceptance of "national communism". His new policy towards Tito in Yugoslavia implemented this change. In the same month Khrushchev dissolved Cominform, the international communist organisation. Communist rule was soon questioned in two satellites in Eastern Europe, Poland and Hungary..

Why do you think the Secret Speech is so important?

- Ideologically Khrushchev announced a major departure from orthodox Marxism-Leninism by introducing the idea of **peaceful co-existence** with the capitalists.

**The Eisenhower administration and the New Look.**

Eisenhower                                              John Foster Dulles

When Eisenhower became the first Republican president for twenty years, he had promised to end the Korean War. But there was no fundamental change in attitude towards communism and no positive response to the new policy in the Kremlin. Eisenhower introduced a new foreign policy which was referred to as **The New Look:**
- Communism should still be contained. Dulles even expressed the desire of a **"roll-back"** of communist controlled areas i.e.a liberation of these areas from communism. Eisenhower supported it but clarified that it had to be achieved by peaceful means and no support was given in Germany in 1953, Poland and Hungary in 1956, when communism was challenged.
- **Nuclear weapons** were now regarded as weapons of first and not last resort. In practical terms this indicated a policy of **massive retaliation** against possible enemies, and less reliance on conventional forces and Truman's policy of fighting "limited wars". As both super powers

were nuclear powers it was a dangerous gamble and Dulles explained this policy of **"brinkmanship"** in a famous interview in 1956:
*"The ability to get to the verge without getting into the war is the necessary art....If you try to run away from it, if you are scared to go to the brink, you are lost."*[29]
- The policy of containment continued by the formation of alliances directed against the communists. In 1954 the South-East Asian Treaty Organisation (**SEATO**) was created by the US, France, Britain, Australia, New Zealand, the Philippines, Thailand and Pakistan, with the main aim of preventing communist expansion in South-East Asia. In 1955 the **Baghdad Pact** was formed between Britain, Iraq and later Iran and Pakistan with the aim of excluding the USSR from the Middle East. The US did not join for tactical reasons but stood behind the organisation. In Europe, Germany was offered full membership status in NATO in 1955 i.e. a decision to allow German troops again. NATO in Europe, SEATO in Asia and The Baghdad Pact in the Middle East surrounded, or *contained* the USSR.

### Why did the US administration not respond to the new signals from the USSR?

- Eisenhower came to power during the war in **Korea** where the Americans had lost 33 000 soldiers due to attacks from two communist states: North Korea and China.
- In 1953, **McCarthy** was at the peak of his career and Eisenhower had won the presidential elections by attacking the Truman administration for being "soft on communism". It was not the right moment for an American "thaw".
- Both Eisenhower and Dulles were **"Cold Warriors"** i.e. strongly anti communists.
- Soviet signs of détente or a thaw were brief and interrupted in 1956 with the crises in **Hungary and the Suez**.


### The Non-aligned movement.

The process of de-colonisation had resulted in a number of newly independent states in the Middle East, Asia and Africa. In 1954 the **Indian Prime Minister Nehru** made a speech discussing Sino (Chinese)-Indian relations. He declared five pillars which should be seen as a guide between the two nations. These pillars would later be the basis of what would be the **Non-Aligned Movement**. The principles were:
- Respect for territorial integrity.
- Mutual non-aggression.
- Mutual non-interference in domestic affairs.
- Equality and mutual benefit.
- Peaceful co-existence.

In 1955 some Asian and African states organised a meeting in **Bandung** in Indonesia. The aims were to promote **Afro-Asian economic and cultural cooperation and to oppose colonialism**. The meeting would play an important role in shaping a Third World identity. To oppose colonialism was in many ways equivalent to a desire to stay out of the Cold War. 29 states representing more than half of the world's population were present. The process of de-colonisation had started and issues that were brought up were France's control of North Africa and the conflict between Indonesia and the Netherlands concerning New Guinea. The conference also supported "the rights of the Arab people of the Palestine". China played a very important role at the conference and her relations with other Asian powers were brought up. The Chinese Prime Minister Zhou Enlai successfully displayed a conciliatory role. One major issue that was brought up was whether Soviet control of Eastern Europe was comparable to Western colonialism. A declaration was made condemning "colonialism in all of its manifestations". The conference called for redistribution of resources for the benefit of poorer states and supported Nehru's principles outlined in 1954.

As a result of the Bandung conference the **Non-aligned Movement was established in Belgrade, Yugoslavia in 1961**. The formation of the organisation was a result of a co-operation between Sukarno from Indonesia, Nasser from Egypt, Nehru from India, Nkrumah from Ghana and Tito from Yugoslavia. 25 states participated. Three questions have dominated the organisation:
- Third World states and their relation to the superpowers i.e. **Cold War issues**. The aim was to find a "third way". It is against this background we see Tito's deep involvement in the organisation.
- **Decolonisation**. The organisation had established itself as an important protest organisation against colonial rule both in Africa and in Asia.
- The third question which dominated later development was the question of a **new economic world order,** i.e how resources should be transferred from richer to poorer countries.

Cold War questions tended to dominate the organisation in the early 60s. In the 1970s, especially after the fourth summit in Algiers in 1973, economic issues and a new world order have dominated. **East-West relations** and conflicts had been replaced by the **North-South conflict**. Tito led the work with Cold War issues while Castro from Cuba was deeply involved in questions about a new economic order. The fact that Cuba, a close ally to the USSR, was deeply involved in the organisation was criticised by some member states. The movement was normally more pro-Soviet than pro-American. The Non-Aligned Movement **lacked economic, military and partly political power** and the member states were very divided.

The importance of the organisation as the **voice of the Third World** should not be neglected. When Soviet leaders discussed whether they should invade Afghanistan in 1979, the Foreign Minster Gromyko opposed the plan and argued: *"All the non-aligned countries will be against us."*[30] Many ideas, especially concerning a new economic world order, have been influential. The idea of a responsibility of richer countries towards the Third World is today widely accepted and the non-aligned movement has been instrumental in this development. One example is the recommendations of the Brandt Commission in 1980.

**Détente interrupted by two crises in 1956:**

**Hungary.**

The Secret Speech started a dangerous political development which challenged Khrushchev's position. What did he say in his speech which gave the satellites this message? Khrushchev talked about how Stalin tried to overthrow Tito:

*"But this did not happen to Tito. No matter how much or how little Stalin shook, not only his little finger but everything else that he could shake, Tito did not fall. Why? The reason was that, in this instance of disagreement with [our] Yugoslav comrades, Tito had behind him a state and a people who had had a serious education in fighting for liberty and independence, **a people who gave support to its leaders**.*
*We have carefully examined the case of Yugoslavia. **We have found a proper solution which is approved by the peoples of the Soviet Union and of Yugoslavia** as well as by the working masses of all the people's democracies and by all progressive humanity. **The liquidation of abnormal relationship** with Yugoslavia was done in the interest of the whole camp of socialism, in the interest of strengthening **peace in the whole world.**"*[31]

Would the USSR now respect a similar relationship with other satellites? Khrushchev should be tested.

The first satellite to react to the Secret Speech was Poland. In June there were riots in **Poznan** and hundreds of workers were wounded by attacking security forces. The Russians and the government responded with a **reform programme and a policy of liberalisation**. Wladislaw Gomulka who had been imprisoned for years after Stalin's purge on "national communists" in the late 40s, was rehabilitated. Khrushchev and the **Russian Politburo** feared too far-reaching reforms in one of the satellites and **went to Poland unexpectedly** in an attempt to avoid a major political crisis. They realised that much had been set in motion by the Secret Speech. There were extremely tense negotiations and the Russians threatened to invade. Gomulka assured the Russian leadership that **no major alterations would be made to the Polish system** i.e. a multi party system would not be allowed and that Poland would still be a member of the Warsaw Pact and remain within the communist camp. But a form of "national communism" had been accepted, collectivisation of agriculture was ended and the regime now sought better relations with the Catholic Church. Gomulka was appointed First Secretary but the Soviet bloc was still considered to be intact.

A more difficult test came only weeks after. In October, 50 000 students, inspired by the development in Poland, demonstrated against communist rule and Soviet control outside the Polish embassy in Budapest. Continuing disorder and political violence soon developed into a **Hungarian uprising against Soviet rule**. The USSR accepted a new government led by Imre Nagy including two non-communists. Dulles made a speech and congratulated the Hungarians for challenging the Red Army. Radio Free Europe, financed by the US, promised US aid. On 27th October a coalition government was formed.

- On 1 November the Nagy government declared that they were **preparing to leave the Warsaw pact, become a neutral country and allow free elections.**

This was a critical moment for Khrushchev and Soviet control of the satellites. If one satellite and Warsaw pact member was allowed to leave, it was very likely that there would be a domino reaction within the Eastern Bloc. Probably the same development that we saw after Gorbachev's new policy was introduced in the late 1980s.
**On 4th November, Soviet forces attacked** Budapest and installed a new pro-soviet government led by Janos Kadar. Imre Nagy was executed and 30,000 Hungarians and 7,000 Russian troops were killed in the uprising. 200,000 Hungarians fled their country and left a gulf of bitterness against Russian rule.

In what way had both Khrushchev's and Eisenhower's policies been tested in the Hungarian crisis?

## The outcome of the Hungarian uprising:

- **The USSR's role as model of communism was questioned** by many communist parties, especially in the west and communist parties in Western Europe lost support.
- Khrushchev and the USSR had drawn a line showing what they could accept in Poland and Hungary. **A disintegration of the satellite system was not going to be tolerated.**
- Domestically, Khrushchev's liberalisation after 1956 was questioned and there was an attempt to overthrow him by old Stalinists in 1957.
- Eisenhower and **the US** had shown that they were not **prepared to risk a war** over territories within the Soviet sphere of influence and that an armed "rollback" was no real alternative.
- It definitely brought an end to the "spirit of Geneva"

**The Suez crisis 1956.**

In 1953 the CIA evaluated Stalin's foreign policy. No attempts had been made to spread communism outside Eurasia. The CIA warned that his successors might not be as cautious. Khrushchev must be seen as more adventurous and when both Czech and Russian arms were sent to Egypt in 1955, it was the first Russian or communist arms agreement with a non-Communist state.
King Farouk of Egypt had been overthrown in an army coup in 1954. Soon **Gamel Abdel Nasser emerged as a new leader**. He was an **Arab nationalist** and opposed both the foundation of the state

of **Israel and traditional Western domination** in the Middle East. As an Egyptian leader he wanted full control of the Suez Canal. These aims and policies soon became a part of the Cold War.
- In 1955 he made an arms deal with the USSR and one of Russia's satellites, Czechoslovakia, and Soviet experts started to train the Egyptian army.
- In 1956 Egypt recognised the communist regime in China. Nasser also concluded an alliance between Egypt, Syria, Saudi Arabia and Yemen, against Israel. Nasser's pro-communist attitude and anti-western propaganda led to the US and Britain cancelling a loan which should finance the building of the Aswan Dam.
- Nasser responded by a **nationalisation of the Suez Canal**.

The Western powers now feared that a strong Nasser would unite the Arabs and pose **a threat to the oil industry, to Israel and allow Soviet influence in the Middle East**. France also wanted to stop the flow of weapons from Egypt to the Algerian nationalists in the crisis which had started in this area. Israel, Britain and France decided to invade Egypt in order to humiliate Nasser and replace him with a pro-western leader.

In October 1956 Israel invaded Egypt and Britain and France bombed Egyptian airfields and sent troops to the area. The invasion met world wide opposition and worst of all, **opposition from both super powers.** Eisenhower could not openly support what could be seen as a colonial aggression and allow the USSR to be the only protector of an Arab state under attack. Khrushchev threatened to intervene militarily. The Security Council passed a resolution calling for a removal of the invading armies to be replaced by UN forces. The US vetoed the International Monetary Fund giving Britain a loan and it faced a financial collapse, Britain surrendered to American demands and called the invasion off. The French had to accept Britain's decision but were furious. Britain and France could do nothing other than accept and Prime Minister Eden in Britain was forced to resign.

**The effects of the Suez crisis.**

- **Nasser's prestige** in the Arab world increased and Arab nationalism grew in strength.
- **Soviet influence in the Middle East grew** and it was Soviet money that financed the Aswan Dam.
- The crisis was disastrous for the traditional British and French influence in the Arab world.
- It diverted attention from the **Hungarian uprising** from which the USSR benefited49greatly.
- In January 1957 Eisenhower launched his **"Eisenhower Doctrine"** and the US Congress gave him the right to provide economic and military assistance to any Middle Eastern country threatened with armed aggression or internal subversion. As a result of this the US intervened in Lebanon in July 1957.
- In July 1958 pro-Nasserite Iraqi army officers murdered the king and the Prime Minister in Iraq and withdrew the country from the Baghdad pact.
- In the late 1950s France started to move away from NATO. A French politician, Pineau, concluded *"the main victim of the (Suez) affair was the Atlantic alliance...if our allies have abandoned us in difficult, even dramatic, circumstances; they would be capable of doing so again if Europe in its turn found itself in danger."*[32] In 1966 the process ended when all French land and air forces were withdrawn from the NATO military command and with the removal of the NATO headquarters from France. France was still a member of NATO. The reasons for De Gaulle's independent foreign policy had several explanations but the Suez crisis was not insignificant.
- Some historians have even argued that the Suez crisis played a role in the process of integrating Europe. On the evening when Britain informed France that she was pulling out, the French foreign minister had a meeting with the German chancellor Adenauer. According to one account Adenauer said: *"There remains to them (i.e. France, Britain and Germany) only one way of playing a decisive role in the world, that is to unite Europe... We have no time to waste; Europe will be your revenge."*[33] The next year the Treaty of Rome, the founding treaty of the European Union, was signed. The French did what they could to keep Britain out of the

union as long as they could. Britain was a close ally to the US and the Suez crisis had shown that this Atlantic relation was more important to Britain than European co-operation. Britain was seen as America's Trojan horse.

> The Cold War had now turned to the Middle East which was an escalation and a departure from Stalinist foreign policy

**Berlin.**

Berlin would once more be a trouble spot in the late 50s and early 60s. The US poured money into West Berlin and soon the city was a **prosperous Western island** contrasting with the areas controlled by the USSR. The worst problem was that many young, educated East Germans fled their country through Berlin and it severely drained the resources of East Germany. It caused a "brain drain". Between 1949 and June 1961, **2,600,000 East Germans fled the country**, an average of more than 200 000 per year. Khrushchev realised that something had to be done. In 1958 he announced that the time had come to find a solution to the Berlin problem:

*"The time has obviously arrived for the signatories of the Potsdam Agreement to renounce the remnants of the occupation regime in Berlin, and thereby make it possible to create a normal situation in the capital of GDR... The USSR...would hand over to the sovereign GDR the functions in Berlin...*[34]

If no solution was reached the USSR would hand over the responsibility for Berlin to the German Democratic Republic. Khrushchev writes in his memoirs: *We were simply asking the other side to acknowledge that two irreconcilable social-political structures existed in Germany...*[35].

This placed the West in a dilemma: if West-Berlin remained as a "free" city but the checkpoints would be handled by East Germans officials, the West would be forced to **deal with a regime** they had promised West Germany not to accept or recognise. The west-Berliners also remembered the days of the Berlin airlift. They could not just accept **giving up West Berlin** or, another alternative, accepting that it should be a demilitarised international area. It would be a devastating signal to other **allies**. Khrushchev gave the Western powers a **six month ultimatum**.
He did not press his point. In 1959 he went to a much published visit to the US and was prepared to once again **postpone his Berlin ultimatum** until a Big Four summit meeting in Paris in May 1960. This summit collapsed on the very first day. In 1956, Eisenhower had authorised reconnaissance spy planes crossing Russian territories. They were out of range of Russian ground-to-air missiles. On 1 May 1960 a US plane was finally shot down by improved missiles and Khrushchev set up a trap. The Russians only announced that a plane had been shot down. The US now claimed it was a weather reconnaissance aircraft, assuming it had not been found. The problem was that the pilot, Gary Powers, survived and explained that he had not swallowed the cyanide capsule as he had been instructed to do. The Russians also had the wreckage of the aircraft and could later put it on display in Moscow with parts of the aircraft, the pilots equipment etc. The incident angered the Russians and Khrushchev demanded a full apology at the Paris summit. Eisenhower accepted full responsibility for this **"U-2 affair"**, but refused to apologise and the Russians left the conference in anger. No solution to the Berlin problem was consequently achieved.

In 1961 the US elected J F Kennedy as president. Khrushchev and the Eastern bloc wanted more than ever a solution to the Berlin problem due to the damaging number of refugees. Khrushchev wrote in his memoirs: *I know there are people who claim that the East Germans are imprisoned in paradise and that the gates of the Socialist paradise are guarded by armed troops. I'm aware that defects exists...*[36] When Kennedy met Khrushchev in **Vienna in June 1961**, he had experienced the fiasco at the **Bay of Pigs** the previous April (see "the Cuban missile crisis") and couldn't abandon this outpost behind the Iron Curtain. Before the summit he said: *"I'll have to show him that we can be as tough as he is..."*[37] No solution was reached but **Khrushchev issued a second six month ultimatum** concerning Berlin. Kennedy asked the Congress for more money to US defence.

In August the uncertainty over Berlin became acute. On 12 August 4,000 people fled the city and the day after the East German government started to erect the **Berlin Wall**, the very symbol of the Cold War. When it happened the situation was very tense and tanks from both sides lined up along the border between the zones in Berlin. Khrushchev wrote in his memoirs:

*"The tanks and troops of both sides spent the night lined up facing each other across the border. It was late October and chilly...."*[38]

The Russians expected an attack but nothing happened. Khrushchev concluded: *"It was a great victory for us..."*[39] For the Russians the problem of refugees was solved but the propaganda value in terms of "badwill" should not be underestimated.

Kennedy had survived his first test after the Bay of Pigs fiasco and he and the Americans had strong support from the West Berliners. In 1963 he went to Berlin and declared in one of the most well known speeches from the Cold War:

*"Freedom is indivisible, and when one man is enslaved, all are not free. When all men are free, then we can look forward to that day when this city will be joined as one, and this country, and this great continent of Europe, in a peaceful and hopeful globe. When that day finally comes, and it will, the people of West Berlin can take sober satisfaction in the fact that they were in the front line for almost two decades.*
*All free men, wherever they may live, are citizens of Berlin, and, therefore, as a free man, I take pride in the words 'Ich bin ein Berliner.'"*[40]

**John F Kennedy**

John F Kennedy was elected US president in the 1960 elections after gaining a narrow margin over Richard Nixon. Kennedy had served on a torpedo boat during W W II and afterwards he wrote a best-seller about Britain's appeasement policy before the war, *"Why England slept"*. His father, Joseph, had been US ambassador to Britain and an outspoken defender of appeasement. Appeasement was the policy where concessions were made to Hitler, to preserve peace. The lesson learned from appeasement was never give in to a dictator. Would this affect Kennedy later?

As a young senator in the early 50s and later as a presidential candidate, he was a dedicated anti-communist. He campaigned vigorously, **attacking the Eisenhower administration** for inadequate defence preparations and especially for allowing a "**missile gap**" to the Soviets. In 1961, Khrushchev boasted that *"The Soviet Union has the world's most powerful rocketry"*[41] which was not true. He also proclaimed that the factories in the USSR were *"turning out missiles like sausages."*[42] It had been a major shock to the Americans when the Soviets had launched the first Sputnik satellite into the space in 1957. Kennedy attacked Eisenhower for being *"second in space, second in missiles."*[43] For a while the Americans were insecure about the size of the nuclear forces in the USSR. As late as 1961 the intelligence service was deeply divided on the question of the missile gap. In his inaugural speech he declared:

*"Let every nation know, whether it wishes us well or ill, that we shall pay any price, bear any burden, meet any hardship, oppose any foe to assure the survival and success of liberty."*[44]

As US president he **increased military spending substantially on both nuclear and conventional forces** by 13 % per year. It was the largest and fastest peacetime military build up in US history. Cuts in conventional forces made by Eisenhower were reversed by Kennedy. Military spending had reached its peak in 1953 when the Korean War ended but was partly reduced throughout the 50s until Kennedy came to power. His new approach in foreign policy was referred to as a policy of **"flexible response"**. The reason behind this policy was that the **communist threat was considered to be more diverse.** Consequently the US must be able to fight a conventional war, a nuclear war with modern technology and to combat revolutionary movements in the Third World. Khrushchev had declared that the ultimate victory of communism would be achieved through **'national-liberation wars'** in the Third World and that he would support such wars whole-heartedly and without reservation. *"The front of the national-liberation movement are multiplying...front of struggle against US imperialism."*[45] The main difference to Eisenhower's policies was less reliance on nuclear weapons. He also attached more emphasis on economic aid as part of a containment policy. This was especially important in the 60s when the decolonisation process in Africa had started.

Kennedy was not a traditional Democrat in his foreign and defence policies, especially if we compare him to the Republican Eisenhower. If we compare the two, Kennedy was the **hawk** and it was Kennedy who undertook a substantial build-up of the US defence system. The ex-general Eisenhower on the other hand had warned the US public of the growth of the "military industrial complex" and in his farewell speech in 1961 he said:

*"This conjunction of an immense military establishment and a large arms industry is new in the American experience. The total influence – economical, political, even spiritual - is felt in every city...every office of the federal government....We must never let the weight of this combination endanger our liberties..."*[46]

It is very informative to study the size of the armies of the superpowers:

Active US Army personnel strength in thousands (source: The Encyclopaedia of American Military):

| | | | |
|---|---|---|---|
| **1936** | **168** | 1951 | 1532 |
| 1938 | 185 | 1953 | 1534 |
| 1942 | 3076 | 1954 | 1405 |
| **1945** | **8268** | **1956** | **1026** |
| 1947 | 991 | 1960 | 871 |
| 1948 | 554 | **1969** | **1510** |
| **1950** | **593** | 1975 | 781 |

The size of the Red Army dropped from 13 million during the war, to **3-5 million during the Cold War**, depending on different Western estimates. Khrushchev continued this reduction in the late 50s and reduced the size of the Red Army from 3,6 to 2,4 million men. Even after this reduction Soviet conventional forces were far stronger than the US army, if we only count the number of soldiers.

There are several interesting thing to notice about these figures. The size of the US army before World War II was smaller than the armies of most European states.

> How is it possible to trace the effects of isolationism before the war in these figures?
> How did World War II affect the number of soldiers in the US and the USSR?
> What was the importance of the Truman Doctrine and the Korean War? (important question)
> How did Eisenhower's New Look affect the size of the army? Why?
> Why did Eisenhower rely more on nuclear weapons? (Help: compare the size of the US and USSR's armies)
> What were the effects of the Vietnam War?

Two things have been most discussed concerning Kennedy's foreign policy: the **Cuban Missile Crisis** and what his intentions in **Vietnam** were.

**The Cuban missile crisis.**

> The main feature of the Cold War was the arms race, especially the nuclear arms race (we will analyse this separately later in this guide). The crisis in Cuba in the early 60s can partly bee seen against this background.

Cuba was liberated from Spain in 1898 and soon a tradition of **US domination** developed, both politically and economically. The US had always seen Latin America as her sphere of influence. The **Monroe Doctrine** from 1823 stated that *"the American continents…are henceforth not be considered as subjects for future colonisations by any European power"* i.e. any attempt by a European power to interfere in the New World was regarded by the US as an unfriendly act. Monroe also stated that *"Our policy in regard to Europe…is not to interfere in the internal concerns of any of its powers."*[47] This tradition of **isolationism** had been established by George Washington in his Farewell Address in 1796 when he advised the US *"to steer clear of permanent alliances with foreign nations…"*[48] The development in America had also been quite peaceful in regards to "wars", except for the US Civil War. Prior to the Second World War, the US army was smaller than the armies in many European states. President James Monroe's declaration in 1823 received little attention at the time but in 1904 **Theodore Roosevelt** announced that the US would interfere in any Latin American country guilty of **"chronic wrong-doing"**: *Chronic wrongdoing, or an impotence which results in a general loosening of the ties of civilized society, may in America, as elsewhere, ultimately require intervention by some civilized nation, and in the Western Hemisphere the adherence of the United States to the Monroe Doctrine may force the United States, however reluctantly, in flagrant cases of such wrongdoing or impotence, to the exercise of an international police power."*[49]

This extension has guided the US to justify intervention many times. In 1947 **the Rio Pact** was signed stating that *"the obligation of mutual assistance and common defence of the American Republics is essentially related to their democratic ideals* and that *an armed attack by any State against an American State shall be considered as an attack against all the American States."*[50] In 1948 **the Organisation of the American States (OAS)** was formed and its charter stated that international communism was incompatible with American freedom. In 1954 the US and CIA had supported and organised a coup in **Guatemala** which led to the overthrow of a regime which had started a land-reform programme. In Guatemala over half the population owned only 3 % of the land but Eisenhower saw the land-reform programme as a first step towards communism.

> Taking the tradition of isolationism in mind and the size of the US army before W W II: what were the effects of the Truman Doctrine, NATO, SEATO and the policies of containment, to the US?

US domination in many areas also led to economic exploitation. This was the situation in Cuba where most of the economy was controlled by American companies. **Half of the land and most of the industry were owned by US companies**. Cuba was led by a right-wing and corrupt **military dictator, Batista**, with the support of the US. Havana was at the time a popular tourist resort infiltrated by US mafia.

- Fidel Castro was a young radical lawyer and a member of the reformist Cuban People's Party. Elections were scheduled for 1952 and Fidel wanted a seat in the House of Representatives. This year Batista carried out a coup which overthrew the government and the **elections were cancelled.**
- Castro now organised an armed opposition and in 1953 he led a suicidal attack on the **Moncada military barracks** with the intention of starting a general revolt, which failed. Castro was sentenced to 15 years imprisonment.
- He was released in 1955 and went to Mexico where Cuban exiles organised **the 26$^{th}$ of July Movement.** 26$^{th}$ of July was the day they had attacked the army barracks. The group declared that they wanted a radical social revolution but didn't declare themselves communists.
- **In 1956 he returned** with 81 men and started to organise a guerrilla war against the Batista regime.
- After two years, in January 1959, Castro's units controlled the country. The **collapse of the regime** and its lack of support becomes clear considering the fact that Castro had 800 guerrillas and the Cuban army officially comprised 30,000 men. Batista fled the country. Castro went to the US in an attempt to get US support, both economically and politically. Eisenhower refused to meet him. Castro had started a **land reform programme and industries were nationalised** but he was still not an outspoken communist.
- In **1960** foreign companies were nationalised step by step. In October the US responded with a **trade embargo**. The US was by far the most important market for Cuban sugar cane and the embargo was a serious threat to the new regime. In the same month all foreign companies were nationalised. **A trade agreement was signed with the USSR** and diplomatic relations and a trade agreement were established with China.

Was it US actions which pushed Castro towards communism or was it a genuine ideological commitment?
**Alternative I**: Castro never declared that he was a communist when he seized power. He did so after the Americans started to attack his new regime. With a trade embargo and sabotage actions by the CIA, the Cuban revolution wouldn't be able to survive. From the beginning, Castro's regime and seizure of power was an attempt to achieve Cuban control of the country, a national liberation. With a US **trade embargo** there was no other alternative. **The US pushed Castro** to the USSR and left no options. In December 1961 he declared that he was a Marxist-Leninist, after the Bay of Pigs.
**Alternative II**: Castro was more than aware of what had happened in Guatemala in 1954. The Arbenz regime in Guatemala had been overthrown by the Americans only because they were suspected communists. If Castro had declared himself a communist from an early stage, he knew that the Americans would never accept such a regime. Consequently **he disguised his beliefs for tactical reasons** in the early stage of the Cuban revolution. But there was no doubt that he was a communist from the beginning.

When Kennedy was elected US president he inherited a plan from the CIA to attack Cuba with the help of Cuban exiles. The US trained the exiles, financed the operation and provided necessary equipment. The idea was that an attack would spur a spontaneous revolt in Cuba. When the plan was implemented at the **Bay of Pigs on 17 April 1961**, everything went wrong and the exiles were easily defeated by the Cuban army. No spontaneous revolt started and when the exiles ran into troubles, no support was given from the US navy. 1,179 Cuban exiles were captured and the US had to pay $ 53 million in baby food and medicine to get them released. Kennedy had to take full responsibility for this devastating fiasco and he was humiliated. It was not a good start for this young and inexperienced president and Cuba became an obsession with him. There was no doubt that Kennedy still wanted to overthrow the Cuban regime. Only three days after the Bay of Pigs he gave Castro a warning that the US government would not hesitate in meeting its primary obligations, the security of the nation. The trade embargo was maintained, the CIA continued with sabotage actions and there was strong political and military pressure from the US. The sabotage actions continued. In 1962 Robert Kennedy said *"no* *time, money, effort – or manpower is to be spared and the budget was over $50 million a year."*[51] Miami was the largest CIA station in the world with 600 full-time CIA officers.

In this situation Castro asked for further military support from the USSR. Khrushchev decided to place nuclear ballistic missiles on Cuba. Why did he do it?

There were three major reasons for the deployment of the missiles:
- He wanted to **protect the Cuban revolution**. The Foreign Minister explained the deployment as a result of *"the very sharp, aggressive stand of the (Kennedy) administration concerning the new Cuba…"*[52]
- The US had 100 intercontinental ballistic missiles (ICBM) and 1,700 intercontinental bombers at the time. The USSR had only 50 ICBMs and 150 bombers. An intermediate range missile in Cuba would reach major cities in the US and compensate for the lack of ICBMs. The USSR was planning to send 40 medium and intermediate-range missiles (IRBM) to Cuba. It would almost double the Soviet nuclear strike capability. In practical terms Khrushchev would **reduce his nuclear inferiority** with the Cuban missiles and it would save an enormous amount of money for the USSR. The alternative, an expensive build-up of Russian ICBM missiles, was extremely costly. The strategic balance would be altered according to the formula IRBM + Cuba = ICBM. Khrushchev wrote in his memoirs: *"In addition to protecting Cuba, our missiles would have equalised what the West likes to call "the balance of power."*[53]
- The US had nuclear missiles in **Turkey**. Khrushchev wrote in his memoirs: *"The United States had already surrounded the Soviet Union with its own bomber bases and missiles. We knew that American missiles were aimed against us in Turkey…"*[54] Eisenhower had concluded in 1959, before the deployment of US missiles in Turkey: *"If Mexico or Cuba had been…began getting arms and missiles from them (the USSR), we would be bound to look on such developments with the gravest concern….(and) take positive actions, even offensive military actions."*[55]

But there were other reasons:
- A communist controlled Cuba would provide the USSR with a springboard to spread communism to underdeveloped countries in Latin America. In the late 50s Khrushchev declared that the ultimate victory of communism would be achieved by war of liberations in the Third World.
- He could claim that he wanted to protect a small state against a superpower. It would strengthen his position in the 3rd World.
- It would put him in a **bargaining position** with the US. "Quid pro quo" i.e. "something in return" was typical for the Cold War. Some kind of solution to the Berlin problem was one possible option. Khrushchev wrote in his memoirs: *"…if Russian blood was shed in Cuba, American blood would surely be shed in Germany."*[56]
- To show toughness to his critics in China and in his own country. Both his domestic and foreign policy were criticised in the Presidium, especially his agricultural policy, the Virgin Land Project, which had failed.

The crisis started when U2 spy-planes established evidence of Soviet medium range missile sites in Cuba on the 14 of October. **Why was this unacceptable to Kennedy**? After all, the Americans had the same type of weapons in Turkey.

- The **Monroe Doctrine** stated that no interference from a European power in America would be tolerated. This policy had been further strengthened by Theodore Roosevelt and his declaration in 1904 of "chronic wrong-doing" and the charter of the OAS and its rejection of communism. A communist Cuba protected by nuclear weapons by its ally USSR was very difficult to accept. This was a **US sphere of influence**.

- Kennedy had attacked Eisenhower for both a "missile gap" and the "loss" of Cuba. It was very difficult from a political point of view to accept a communist nuclear build-up so close to the US. An intermediate-range ballistic missile in Cuba would reach the US's major cities. **Politically this could not be tolerated**. From a strict security perspective the importance of this can be questioned. The Russians had 50 intercontinental ballistic missiles (ICBM) and some 150 intercontinental bombers and could destroy the US anyway. Robert McNamanra, the Secretary of Defence concluded: *"A missile is a missile. It makes no difference whether you are killed by a missile fired from the Soviet Union or from Cuba."* He also concluded: *"I don't think there is a military problem here....This is a domestic, political problem."*[57] There should be mid-term **election to the Congress** in November the same year. Another Cuban "fiasco" would be devastating, politically to Kennedy and his Democratic Party. The Kennedy brothers even thought that if they had not reacted the President might run the risk of being impeached by the Republicans. The President told his brother on his way to an Ex Comm meeting: *"I would have been impeached."*[58]

**The 13 Days of the Crisis:**

US reconnaissance photograph from Cuba    Excomm meeting 29 October 1962

---

You may see different terms describing medium-range missiles. The problem is that various terms are used by different countries, making definitions about medium range missiles is subjective and arbitrary. A **Medium-Range Ballistic Missile**, abbreviated **MRBM** is defined by the US Department of Defense as having a maximum range of between 1,000-3,000 km in other words a short range missile. The **SS- is an MRBM** and what started the crisi when it was discovered on 14/10,. An **Intermediate-Range Ballistic Missile, IRBM** according to the US definition is a ballistic missile with a range of 3,000-5,500 km and would reach the US west coast. i.e. a long-range missile. IRBM sites under constuction were discovered on 17/10. It is doubtful if any IRBMs reached Cuba at any time but it was planned and sites **under construction** were discovered.

**14 October:** **U2 spy-planes** established evidence of a Soviet medium range missile base in Cuba.
**16 October:** The **ExComm** – a group of advisers was formed.
Possible solutions to the crisis:
- Invasion i.e. a direct confrontation with the Red Army.
- A "surgical" air strike which could be followed by an invasion. It was turned down because an air strike would not destroy all missiles.
- A **blockade,** or a 'quarantine', i.e. a naval blockade to prevent the USSR from sending components for the missiles to Cuba. It would give time for a diplomatic solution but what would happen when the Russian ships met the US marines? Was it the start of World War III?

**22 October** Kennedy gave a dramatic **TV speech** to the nation and announced the existence of nuclear weapons 90 miles away from Florida and the US **blockade.**

**24 October** One of the most dramatic days, when the **Russian ships finally turned back**. The US Secretary of State Dean Rusk said: *"We were eyeball to eyeball, and I think the other fellow just blinked."*[59]

**26 October:** Khrushchev sent Kennedy **a message** where he offered to withdraw the missiles if the US promised never to invade Cuba. The same day a US **U2 spy plane was shot down** over Cuba and the pilot was killed. Several advisers now recommended an assault on Cuba. What the Americans didn't know was that the nuclear weapons on Cuba where already operational and that the Russian military commander had been authorised to use nuclear weapons in self defence without consulting Moscow. This was a very critical day.

**27 October:** Khrushchev sent a **second message** where a deal now must include the removal of NATO missiles in **Turkey**. Robert Kennedy now secretly met the Russian ambassador Dobrynin and an agreement about the Turkish missiles was made, but it had to remain secret. Kennedy was aware that a removal required consultations within NATO and there was no time for that, a deal *"could break up the (NATO) Alliance by confirming European suspicions that we would sacrifice their security to protect our interests."*[60] He was also not willing to officially admit that he had made such a commitment as a result of Soviet pressure.

Two days later, on the **28 October** Khrushchev informed Kennedy via Radio Moscow (!) that USSR had accepted the terms. Castro had not been informed and refused a UN inspection of the dismantling of the missiles.

The solution of the crisis:
- The USSR would **remove the missiles**.
- A US pledge to **never invade Cuba**.
- US Jupiter missiles should be removed from Turkey. This was not made public.

Officially it was **Kennedy who gained** politically from the crisis. He had made the Russians withdraw the missiles without a war. He had also been able to handle the internal pressure from warmongers, without starting a war. **Khrushchev** on the other hand was **criticised** not only in the USSR but he was also bitterly attacked by Mao in China. In 1964 he was forced to resign and even if according to the indictment against him it was mainly due to domestic reasons, the Cuban crisis played a role. He was blamed for *"erratic leadership, of taking hasty and ill-considered actions."* [61] The Red Army, which had been substantially reduced by Khrushchev earlier, found the dismantling of the missiles in Cuba humiliating.

But there are several flaws in these conclusions. **Few or no one knew about the Turkish deal.** It is also clear that the US pledge to **never invade Cuba was a substantial victory to Khrushchev**. Kennedy's initial aim had been a withdrawal without any conditions. So by placing missiles in Cuba Khrushchev was able to secure the Cuban revolution and to remove missiles from Turkey. Another point worth considering is the responsibility for bringing the world to the verge of a nuclear war. It is generally believed by historians, still today, that this is the closest we have been to a nuclear war. Who was responsible for this?

**Khrushchev** was responsible for the decision to place nuclear weapons on Cuba. Formally it was the Presidium, the highest organ of the Communist Party in 1962 (it was the Politburo which was called Presidium between 1952-1966), which made the decision but it was Khrushchev's idea from the beginning and he was powerful enough to impose his will on the decision makers. He should have been aware of how serious this must have been to an American President. It was not only the tradition of the Monroe doctrine. Central America and the Caribbean was a **US "sphere of influence"** and it was a very dangerous game to surprise your enemy with nuclear weapons in such an area. Khrushchev wrote in his memoirs: *"I had the idea of installing missiles with nuclear warheads in Cuba without letting the United States find out that they were there until it was too late to do anything about them".*[62] Cuba within a US sphere of influence was not comparable to Turkey. The Security adviser McGeorge Bundy said *"we felt the same way you would feel if we put missiles in Finland."*[63] The US had their suspicions and Kennedy warned Khrushchev before the crisis that the US would prevent the installation of Soviet nuclear weapons by whatever means might be necessary. Khrushchev had replied that *"we do not have any bases in Cuba"* and *"we do not intend to establish any."*[64]

**Kennedy** on the other hand had put enormous pressure on Cuba with the trade embargo, the Bay of Pigs invasion and sabotage in the Mongoose operation and this pressure was one of the main reasons for nuclear aid to Cuba. In 1962 the US Senate had passed a resolution by 86-1, calling for the use of force, if necessary, to stop Cuban aggression and communist activities in the Western hemisphere. It can also be argued that the US had no right to object to what the Russians were doing in Cuba due to the simple fact that they **were doing the same in Turkey,** or to use Khrushchev's own words: *"The Americans had surrounded our country with missile bases....now they would learn just what it feels like to have enemies' missiles pointing at you."*[65] It can also be questioned if Soviet missiles in Cuba was a serious threat to US security and the real reason for Kennedy's actions. McNamara suggested that *"I don't think there is a military problem here....This is a domestic, political problem."*[66] After his elections campaign attacking Eisenhower and after the Bay of Pigs, Kennedy couldn't afford to look like a **weak president.** The mid term elections to the Congress in November played a role. A second Cuban fiasco would be devastating for the Democrats. This domestic political factor probably affected his decision-making.

The escalation of the crisis, the blockade and spy planes over Cuba, were Kennedy's decisions. It is a very strong case to argue that a **blockade** on international water against one state is illegal and that Kennedy was responsible for the crisis. Nuclear weapons were already in Cuba when Kennedy risked world peace by setting up this blockade.

Mikhail Gorbachev later concluded that both were to blame: *"The Cuban Missile crisis reminds me of two boys fighting in the schoolyard over who has the bigger stick."*[67]

---

Historiography:
**Orthodox historians** or traditionalists like Arthur Schlesinger Jr and insiders like Theodor Sorensen (i.e. pro-Kennedy), argue that the missiles were an intolerable provocation and that Kennedy responded due to a desire to defend **legitimate security needs**, to preserve **NATO** and show American **credibility**. The **quarantine was a successful** strategy and Kennedy was a skilful leader in times of crisis.
**Revisionists** like I. F. Stone and Ronald Steel argue that Kennedy, with his background attacking the Eisenhower administration for the loss of Cuba, risked a war over Cuba for **domestic political gains**. Confrontation would make it possible to get the missiles out before the November **elections**. But it was not only a question of electoral and political pressure. Kennedy also risked a **revolt from the military** and other hardliners in different departments. The **blockade was irresponsible** and Kennedy is seen as neurotic. The US also has to take the blame for the deployment of **missiles in Turkey** which led to the Cuban affair.

**What were the consequences of the crisis?**

- The US was forced to tolerate a **communist state in the Caribbean**.
- The time had come for a **more constructive dialogue**. The crisis had a profound sobering effect on the nuclear powers.
- A **Test Ban Treaty** was signed in 1963 forbidding nuclear testing in the atmosphere.
- A **Hot Line**, a direct telephone line, was established between the White House and the Kremlin.
- **Khrushchev** was criticised not only by Mao in China but also in Moscow. In 1964 he was forced to resign. In Pravda he was criticised for being "hare-brained" and supporting "wild schemes, half-baked conclusions and hasty decisions". The Cuban crisis was one factor behind his **dismissal**.
- In a longer perspective it led to renewed **Soviet efforts to close the missile gap**. The consequence was an extensive and very expensive Soviet nuclear build-up which would have far reaching consequences to the Soviet economy.

> The last point is often ignored. It is normally argued that the aftermath of the crisis led to a period of détente. This is true if we focus upon the immediate consequences. But it must be emphasised that the USSR leaders decided never to be humiliated again due to nuclear weakness. The USSR decided, partly as a consequence of the Cuban crisis, to close the only missile gap that existed i.e. Soviet inferiority. Let's study the nuclear balance after the crisis over a longer period:

ICBM = intercontinental ballistic missile
SLBM = submarine launched ballistic missile
ICB = intercontinental bombers

source: Cold war to Détente by Brown/Mooney p. 161

|      |      | 1964 | 1966 | 1968 | 1970 | 1972 |
|------|------|------|------|------|------|------|
| US   | ICBM | 834  | 904  | 1054 | 1054 | 1054 |
|      | SLBM | 416  | 592  | 656  | 656  | 656  |
|      | ICB  | 630  | 630  | 545  | 550  | 455  |
| USSR | ICBM | 200  | 300  | 800  | 1300 | 1527 |
|      | SLBM | 120  | 125  | 130  | 280  | 560  |
|      | ICB  | 190  | 200  | 150  | 150  | 140  |

By 1972 the Soviets had finally **closed the missile gap**, and even had an advantage. How much was this policy **a result of the Cuban crisis**? It is of course a very difficult question to answer but many historians argue that this build-up was a result of the Cuban crisis. What we do know for sure is that **the cost** of this programme was something that would severely affect Russian society.

The costs for the nuclear arms race were astronomical to both sides. In the 1980s the US produced five nuclear warheads per day.[68] What was achieved from a security point of view? Gaddis writes:

*"...McNamara insisted that a 17-1 advantage for the US in 1962 still translated into an effective nuclear parity because the prospect of only a few nuclear explosions on American soil would deter Washington from doing anything that might provoke them."*[69]

## Cuba and the Cold War after the crisis.

> Questions about the importance of Cuba on Cold War development are quite common in IB exams. You need to write more than just about the missile crisis. The most important "Cuban" Cold War events will now be outlined. Another alternative is to use Cuba as an example in an "open question" like "Examine the impact of the Cold War on two countries…." Cuba may be a useful example if you prepare for it.

Even if the crisis had led to a peaceful solution, the US remained an extremely hostile neighbour. The **economic embargo was not lifted** which affected Cuba. In 1961 Kennedy had authorised a covert plan called "Operation Mongoose" resulting in **sabotage actions**. These kinds of actions continued after the crisis.

Did the Americans have any reason to fear Castro? Castro, with the support of the USSR, wanted to inspire other countries in **Latin America** to turn to communism. He had ideological reason for this but it would also end Cuba's isolation in the region. There were revolutionary groups in Latin America receiving both training and weapons from Cuba. The most well known is Castro's friend and ex-minister Che Guevara. Both **Che Guevara** and Castro hoped to inspire "**many Vietnams**", a small nation fighting a non-conventional war against the Americans, but now in Latin America. In 1965 Che left Cuba to support a revolutionary group in Bolivia but was captured and shot in 1967. The attempts to spread the revolution in Latin America didn't succeed but these Cuban inspired attempts worried the US.

The US trade embargo made Castro more or less totally dependent on Soviet aid. Consequently he was loyal to the USSR and supported the Warsaw Pact's invasion of Czechoslovakia in 1968. Castro was also an internationalist and the de-colonisation process in Africa gave him an opportunity to show this commitment. In 1974 there was a revolution in Portugal. The year after, Portuguese colonies were granted independence, Mozambique, Guinea-Bissau and Angola. In **Angola** a bitter civil war started between the MPLA, FNLA and UNITA. These organisations were backed by several foreign states and MPLA was backed by the USSR. The FNLA was backed by the US, i.e. decolonisation became a part of the Cold War. To Castro the decolonisation and a struggle for national liberation from foreign control, was a known experience. Cuba intervened militarily and sent **17 000 Cuban troops** who were shipped by the Russians to support the MPLA in the civil war in Angola. The MPLA seized power in Angola and signed a friendship treaty with the USSR in 1976. Mozambique did the same the following year. In 1977 Castro again sent about **17 000 combat troops** to another conflict in Africa: the Ethiopian government wanted to expel Somalia from the Ogaden region. **Ethiopia** soon became a pro-Russian state.

Castro's involvement in the decolonisation process and his support for world revolution kept the conflict with the US alive. No possible détente with the US was in sight. But by supporting her Soviet ally in further globalisation of the Cold War in the Third World, Cuba would strengthen her bonds with the Russians upon whose support the **Cuban economy was so dependent**.

In **1979** a revolution broke out in Nicaragua in Central America. The Sandinistas, a coalition of Marxists, other radicals, and liberals, overthrew Anastasio Somoza after a guerrilla war. Somoza was considered as a corrupt leader even by President Carter in the US and close to a human disaster. There was much international support for the new regime which received substantial aid from many countries in Western Europe but soon also 2 500 advisors from Cuba. The aim of the new regime was to create a mixed economy and social and economic justice. The Carter administration also gave some aid in the beginning. With the advent of Reagan as President in January 1981 the situation changed and the US started to support the Contras, a right-wing group fighting the regime in Nicaragua. In 1983 the US invaded the small Caribbean island of **Grenada,** to overthrow a left-wing regime. Reagan claimed that the regime was turning the island into a "**Soviet-Cuban colony**". There were both Cuban and North Korean advisers in Grenada who were overwhelmed by the Americans. When the Grenada invasion took place, the regime in Nicaragua urged the regime in Havana (!) to recall its advisers in Nicaragua. It was believed that the Cuban presence might trigger a US invasion of Nicaragua, hence the few Cubans had a major impact.

The developments in Nicaragua and Grenada are important events from a Cold War perspective. But Cuban activities in these two conflicts were of **minor importance.** The very fact that attention was paid to Cuba in these conflicts shows the importance of Cuba in Cold War relations.

**The Congo crisis 1960-64**

The period after W. W. II. witnessed a process by which European colonies in Africa and Asia became fully independent states. In 1946 there were 51 countries represented in the United Nations and today there are 204, which to a major extent can be explained by this process of decolonisation. There are many aspects in this development which can be discussed, but in this context it will be discussed from a Cold War perspective. If the Suez crisis in the 1950s made it clear that the Cold War now also involved the Middle East, the Korean war and the Indo-China war showed that Asia was also a Cold War battle ground. The Congo crisis in the early 1960s and the wars in Angola and Ethiopia in the 1970s clearly showed that Africa also was a focus of Cold War tension.

Congo was given independence from Belgium in June 1960. The country was led by prime minister Patice Lumumba and president Joseph Kasavubu. Only a few weeks after the independence the government ran into difficulties when the army mutinied against their Belgian officers. Acts of violence were committed against remaining Belgian and European residents and the Belgian government decided, against the will of the Congo government, to send paratroopers to protect the 100, 000 European residents who lived in the country.

In the southern part of the country, in the Katanga province, a rival force led by Moise Tshombe also challenged the government. The province was incredibly rich in natural resources and Tshombe was soon supported by European investors and industrialists.

In this very problematic situation the Lumumba government appealed to the UN. The UN decided in resolution 143 to send troops to Congo to stabilise the situation. The resolution also made it clear that the UN would not take sides in the conflict. Lumumba's aim had been to get UN help in defeating Tshombe and his faction in the south. Lumumba accused the UN for siding with the Europeans or Western powers and turned to the USSR for help. Lumumba received massive military aid from the USSR and about a thousand Soviet technical advisers within six weeks. Lumumba now launched an attack on Tshombe in the south which proved unsuccessful. This caused major problems for the president and the army chief of staff, Mobutu. The Americans saw the Soviet activity as an attempt to spread communist influence in Congo. Mobutu came under great pressure. Western nations, which helped pay the soldiers' salaries, as well as Kasavubu and Mobutu's subordinates, favoured getting rid of the Soviet presence. Kasavubu's solution was to dismiss Lumumba.

The disintegration of the new state escalated when president Kasavubu decided to remove Lumumba. Lumumba had strong support in the eastern provinces and he was also reinstated by the parliament in the country. The USSR continued to support him with weapons. On 14 September 1960 Mobutu took control in a CIA-sponsored coup. Lumumba was placed under house arrest and Kasavubu was kept as president. Lumumba was publicly beaten and forced to eat copies of his speeches. He disappeared and it has later been revealed that he was murdered the same day. In 1961 four different groups claimed that they wanted to establish political control of the country and it looked like the country was heading for a full scale civil war. Finally the UN decided to pass a resolution which gave their forces the right to use force. In this situation three of four factions fighting for the control of Congo convened to form a new government under Cyrille Adoula. In August 1961 5 000 troops started an attack on Katanga and took full control of the province in 1963. Another rebellion led by Pierre Mulele was crushed between 1964-65.

The UN had been able to take action but was criticised by many states, especially the USSR and Belgium. The UN Secretary, General Dag Hammardkjold, died in a plane crash when he visited the region. Both superpowers had been involved in the crisis and it has been argued that the CIA was involved in the assassination of the pro-Soviet Lumumba. The CIA also supported Mobutu when he seized power in 1965. Mobutu ruled the country (renamed Zaire) between 1965 and 1996. His regime is normally described as both corrupt and brutal but he remained in power for such a long time due to the fact that he was supported by the US, which was very important during the Cold War. The fact that he finally lost power to the opposition leader Laurent Kabila in 1996, should also be seen in the light of the Cold War coming to an end. Western support evaporated and he was accused of corruption and human rights abuses.

## The war in Indo China.

> This conflict will be outlined in more in detail in the next part of this guide as it ended in the mid 70s. It is of vital importance to discuss its consequences if you want to understand this event in a Cold War perspective. But a brief summary must be made when we are discussing the 50s and the 60s, in order to get an appropriate overview of this period.

The power vacuum left by the Japanese after W. W . II led to Ho Chi Minh being able to declare the independence of the People's Republic of Vietnam in 1945. This was opposed by the French who were keen to re-establish their colonies in South East Asia. In 1946 a full scale war started between the Viet Minh (the Vietnam League for Independence) and the French. When the French left Vietnam in 1954 the war had killed 110,000 French soldiers, which is many more casualties than the Americans suffered in their Vietnam War. They lost 58,000 soldiers. When the French left, the Americans were paying 70 % of the French cost for the war.

The late 1950s was a relatively calm period in the area, partly due to the fact that Ho carried out a land reform in the North. In the early 1960s the Viet Cong, the guerrilla movement in the South, intensified its activities. When Kennedy came to power there were 400 US advisers in Vietnam and by the time he was assassinated in 1963, it had increased to 16 000. But it was Johnson who escalated the conflict. After a naval incident in the Gulf of Tonking in 1964 the Congress accepted giving the president the right to *"take all necessary steps, including the use of armed force."*[70] to defend South Vietnam. The President could now escalate the conflict without a formal declaration of war. This "blank cheque" was used by Johnson and in 1965 there were 180,000 US troops in Vietnam and in 1968 the number had increased to 540,000 men. Johnson also started air bombing the North.

When Nixon came to power in 1968 he realised that US involvement was probably not going to assure victory and he was also worried about the development of the US economy. He started a policy of "Vietnamisation" to make the South Vietnamese take more responsibility and step by step withdraw US troops. In 1971 there were 157 000 US soldiers in Vietnam and in 1973 a ceasefire was agreed.

If we look at the 1950s and the 60s there are two major consequences of the French and the American Vietnam wars (or the Indochina war and the Vietnam war):

International implications of the Indochina and Vietnam War in the 50s and 60s.

- The conflict between the French and Viet Minh in Indochina together with the "loss" of China and the Korean War, deeply affected US foreign policy. The Viet Minh were supported by China from the early 50s. and there was a fear that if Vietnam was lost, the rest of South East Asia would be lost, the Domino Theory. In 1954 the South-East Asian Treaty Organisation (**SEATO**) was created by the US, France, Britain, Australia, New Zealand, the Philippines, Thailand and Pakistan, with the **main aim of preventing communist expansion in South-East Asia**.
- The formation of SEATO deeply worried Mao in China and Jiang, the leader of Taiwan, now announced a "holy war against communism". This development is probably the reason for China starting to shell some small **islands controlled by Taiwan in 1954 and 1955**. This is referred to as the Taiwan Straits Crisis. During this crisis the US threatened to use nuclear arms against China in line with Eisenhower's policy of "massive retaliation". It drew the US and Taiwan closer, signing a **mutual defence pact**. The USSR on the other hand made it clear to Mao that no Soviet support would be given to a Chinese attack on Taiwan. This contributed to the growing **split between China and the USSR**

Implications in the 1960s:

- When one of the superpowers was involved in a conflict which engaged more that 500 000 soldiers, it had major consequences. The US economy and the dollar suffered severely and it brought an end to the Bretton Woods system, a monetary system where the dollar was placed on the Gold Standard and the most important currencies in the Western World were fluctuating against the dollar. The fact that no victory was achieved, soldiers were killed and the economy suffered, made the US and Nixon approach both the USSR and China. The US would not be able to maintain its economic and military superiority if the war was not brought to an end. If the US could not contain China in Asia, and that became more and more clear with the Vietnam War, she had to come to turns with this. A new **policy of détente and linkage** was a policy where the US was prepared to respect Soviet sphere of influences and offer the USSR Western technology, if the USSR co-operated in attempts to end the Vietnam War. The late 60s saw the beginning of détente between the US and the USSR. The Vietnam War was also one reason behind Nixon's visit to China in 1972, the beginning of a US-Chinese rapprochement. A Cold War triangle had been created.

> US involvement in Vietnam created a US reluctance to be involved in further military conflicts in the Third World. This was something that the Russians took advantage of in the 1970s. This will be further outlined in the part where we discuss the 70s.

**The Sino Soviet split.**

Mao in 1946                                         Portrait of Chairman Mao at the Tiananmen Gate

The split between the two leading communist states developed in the late 50s. It had many reasons. Mao was in many ways a **Chinese nationalist** and didn't want China to be just another Russian satellite. There had been problems during the Civil War when Stalin temporarily **supported the Nationalists**. He wanted a strong China to oppose Japan and believed that the Nationalists were the alternative. There were also **ideological reasons** for the split as Mao claimed that a socialist revolution doesn't have to occur in an industrialised society based on industrial workers. Mao emphasised that the Chinese revolution was a peasant based revolution. Mao also felt that the **terms offered by the USSR in the Sino Soviet Friendship treaty of 1950**, were not favourable to China. The co-operation was more a result of necessity due to the weakness of China after the Civil War and her involvement in the Korean War. During the **Taiwan crises** in 1954-55 the Russians made it clear that no Russian support could be expected if China attacked Taiwan. After the **Secret Speech** in 1956, relations soon deteriorated. Mao saw Khrushchev's speech as an indirect attack on himself and he didn't support the new policy of **peaceful co-existence**. The USSR was also reluctant to provide Mao with an **atomic bomb**. In 1959 the USSR suddenly withdrew Russian technicians and advisers. The same year there were border disputes and armed clashes between China and India and the USSR remained neutral. There was not <u>one</u> communist camp under the leadership of Moscow. The **importance of**

**personalities** has also been emphasised by some historians. Khrushchev and Mao did not get along very well together.

It would take many years until this new situation had an effect on the Cold War. In the 1960s during the Cultural Revolution China went through a period where she was isolated and had no close relation to any superpower. When she decided to end her isolation she actually turned to the US. This so called ping-pong diplomacy established a Cold War triangle. More about this later.

## The Prague Spring.

If there were signs of a better understanding after the Cuban crisis there were also signs of tension and major crisis. The US escalation in Vietnam in 1965 was of major importance. The next crisis would occur in Europe when Czechoslovakia announced a reform policy in 1968. The Soviets had consolidated their power in Eastern Europe between 1945-48 and established a firm control in every country except Yugoslavia. In 1953, when Stalin died, there had been a revolt in Berlin against Soviet control, which was crushed by tanks. After the Secret Speech in 1956 two of the satellites wanted more independence from Moscow. The Poles' desire for more independence was finally accepted because it didn't challenge Soviet power in vital areas. But when the Hungarians announced that they were going to accept free elections and to leave the Warsaw pact, Russian tanks entered Budapest. In 1960 Albania had also been able to establish independence from Moscow.

It would take twelve years after Hungary until Soviet power was again challenged. Czechoslovakia was the most industrially advanced country within the Eastern bloc. It had however faced economic difficulties in the 60s and in 1967 student demonstrations had been brutally suppressed. In January 1968 **Alexander Dubcek** became First Secretary of the Communist Party. In April an "Action Programme" was announced promising freedom of speech, a free press, the right to travel abroad and freedom for political parties within the Communist controlled National Front. The aim was to create **"socialism with a human face".** This development alarmed both Moscow and other Warsaw pact leaders. Several meetings and warnings were given to Dubcek. After a meeting in Warsaw an open letter was issued from five Warsaw Pact leaders, including the USSR. It warned the Czechs that counter-revolutionaries threatened the existence of socialism in the country: *"...we believe that a decisive rebuff to the forces of anti-communism....in Czechoslovakia is not only your task but ours too."*[71] Dubcek and the Czech leaders repeatedly assured their loyalty to both socialism and the Warsaw Pact but continued with the reforms. In August plans were announced that would allow a multi party system.

On the 20th of August 1968 the five signatories of the Warsaw letter invaded Czechoslovakia. It was met by massive hostility and passive resistance i.e. no new Hungary. The invasion brought an end to the Prague Spring.

Consequences for the Cold War:

- The Prague Spring **only temporarily** halted the process of détente. Johnson made it clear that no interference from the US was expected and consequently the détente process which had only partly begun, could continue. The Vietnam problem, which might involve Russian co-operation to be solved, was more important.
- In November 1968 Brezhnev announced his **Brezhnev Doctrine**: *"When internal and external forces hostile to Socialism attempt to turn the development of any Socialist country in the direction of the capitalist system...(it) becomes not only a problem for the people of that country but also a general problem, the concern of all Socialist countries."*[72] What the Soviets now announced was that they believed that if one country fell from socialism, all others would do it. This would give the socialist countries the right to intervene.
- China, who had supported the crushing of the Hungarian uprising in 1956, condemned the invasion of Czechoslovakia. We can see the beginning of a "Cold War triangle".

# Student activities 2.

We have already stated that 1953-69 was marked by both confrontation and détente. What was also typical was that the Cold War expanded into new areas. Both the Middle East and The American continent were now involved in the Cold War. If we should make an attempt to divide different events from the period we can see how confrontation and détente were replacing each other. This is partly a simplification, and some other events can be included, but it is possible to conclude that there was both confrontation and détente during this period.

| Détente | Confrontation |
|---|---|
| 1953 an armistice was signed in Korea. The new leadership in the USSR started to talk about peaceful co-existence. | In the US it was the McCarthy years and Eisenhower announced his "New Look" and "massive retaliation". |
| 1954 Peace conference in Geneva about Vietnam | 1954 SEATO formed, problems in Taiwan. |
| 1955 End of occupation of Austria. 1955 Summit in Geneva, "The spirit of Geneva". | 1955 Germany a full member of NATO and The Warsaw pact formed. |
| 1956 The Secret Speech. Talks about "national roads to socialism" and peaceful co-existence. | 1956 Problems in Poland and a revolt in Hungary. The Suez crisis. |
|  | 1958 Khrushchev's Berlin ultimatum. |
| 1959 Khrushchev to the US. | 1959 Castro to power |
|  | 1960 the U2 incident and the Paris summit |
|  | 1961 Berlin Wall and the Bay of Pigs |
|  | 1962 The Cuban Missile crisis. After the crisis the USSR started to close "the missile gap". |
| 1963 The Hot Line, the Test Ban Treaty. |  |
|  | 1964 The Gulf of Tonkin resolution |
|  | 1965 US escalation in Vietnam |
| 1967 The signing of a treaty on demilitarisation of space. | 1968 The Prague Spring. |

**Answer the following questions before working with the essay outlines:**

1. How did the new leadership in the Kremlin temporarily change Soviet foreign policy after 1953?

_____
_____
_____
_____
_____

2. Describe Eisenhower's foreign policy.

_____
_____
_____
_____

3. Why is the Secret Speech from 1956 so important?

_____
_____
_____
_____

4. What was the Non Aligned Movement and what importance did it have on the Cold War?

5. Why was the Hungarian uprising a test of both Khrushchev and Eisenhower?

6. What were the results of the Suez crisis?

7. What were the reasons for the Sino-Soviet split?

8. What role did Berlin play in the Cold War in the late 50s and early 60s?

9. Why did the Indo China war start?

10. Describe Khrushchev's foreign policy in the late 50s.

11. Describe Kennedy's foreign policy in the early 60s.

12. Why did Khrushchev place missiles in Cuba in 1962?

13. How and why did Kennedy respond?

14. How was the crisis solved and who do you think "won"?

15. What were the consequences?

16. Why was the Vietnam War escalated in the early 60s and what was the Gulf of Tonking resolution?

17. What was the Brezhnev doctrine?

**We will now present a number of eassay outlines in order to get an overview and to highlight some issues:**

7. How were the Truman Doctrine and the policy of containment implemented in the period 1947-61?
8. Why and with what results did the USSR place missiles in Cuba in 1962?
9. Why has Cuba been an important country in Cold War history?
10. Why was Germany a centre of Cold War problems in the years 1945-61?
11. "The Asian development of the Cold War was far more dangerous than the European development". With reference to events from the period 1945-60, how far do you agree?
12. "It is unjustified to see Khrushchev as a Cold Warrior". Do you agree?

Essay Title: **7. How were the Truman Doctrine and the policy of containment implemented in the period 1947-61?**

Introductory points:

Conclusion:

**7. How were the Truman Doctrine and the policy of containment implemented in the period 1947-61?** *(It is a list question. Go through chronologically how it was implemented and don't forget to define and explain the Truman Doctrine and the containment policy in the beginning)*

**Containment** was the US policy that was adopted by President Truman in his Truman Doctrine in 1947 by which the US attempted **to prevent further Soviet or communist expansion** beyond territories occupied in 1945. No long-term co-operation with the USSR was possible and the intellectual basis had been provided by George Kennan in his Long Telegram from 1946. By supporting the "free world" mainly militarily but also economically, like the Marshall Plan in Europe and economic aid to Japan, the expansion of communism would be prevented. To prevent the expansion of communism resulted in the building of military alliances surrounding the communists.

**The Truman Doctrine** stated that it should be US policy to support nations who are fighting an internal or external communist threat. Initially intended only for Greece and Turkey but soon extended globally. Not only military means were used. Economical means, like the Marshall Plan, could be used.

There is a lot of information so don't overwrite. Dealing with a question where you may know too many points requires that you emphasise your main points and briefly mention points of minor importance. The most important points are:

1. Help was given both to **Greece and Turkey** and they remained within the Western camp
2. Truman was able to pass the Marshall Plan through the Congress in 1948. The effect of the Marshall Plan is normally considered as **successful** and led to a massive industrial growth with a GNP growth in Europe of around 15-25% annually.
3. From the late 40s substantial aid was given to **Japan** to build a stronghold against communism in Asia.
4. Through the **Berlin airlift** Berlin was saved from a communist takeover.
5. Germany was given both economic and political support. In 1949 the **independence of West Germany** was proclaimed and she received substantial economic aid.
6. In April 1949 **NATO** was founded. Twelve states joined the organisation and according to article 5, "an armed attack against one or more …… be considered an attack on them all". Germany became a full member in 1955.
7. In 1950 there was full support for **South Korea** when they were attacked by the North.
8. To achieve containment and to stop the expansion of communism the **NSC-68 report** was implemented from 1950. It led to a massive US military build up.
9. Containment and the Truman doctrine were now implemented in Asia. The US started to support the French in the **Indochina War** and support was also given to protect **Taiwan**. The build up of Japan was strengthened.
10. With Eisenhower a partly new foreign policy was introduced called the "New Look". However this policy was in essence not different. The aim was to prevent the spread of communism globally and to contain it. The talk about "roll-back" proved to be rhetorical.
11. In 1954 the South-East Asian Treaty Organisation (**SEATO**) was created by the US, France, Britain, Australia, New Zealand, the Philippines, Thailand and Pakistan, with the main aim of preventing communist expansion in South-East Asia.
12. In 1955 the **Baghdad Pact** was formed between Britain, Iraq and later Iran and Pakistan with the aim of excluding the USSR from the Middle East. The US didn't join this pact but unofficially clearly supported it
13. In January 1957 Eisenhower launched his **"Eisenhower Doctrine"**: the US Congress gave him the right to provide economic and military assistance to any Middle East country threatened with armed aggression or internal subversion. As a result of this the US intervened in Lebanon in July 1957.
14. Full support was given to **Berlin 1958-61**.
15. Trade embargo against **Cuba** and the Bay of Pigs in 1961. 15.000. US advisers in Vietnam.

**Conclusion:** Summarise your main points

Essay Title: **8. Why and with what results did the USSR place missiles in Cuba in 1962?**

Introductory points:

Conclusion:

**8. Why and with what results did the USSR place missiles in Cuba in 1962?** *(There is nothing complicated here: list the reasons why the USSR decided to place missiles in Cuba and account for the consequences)*

**Why?**

1. The USSR wanted to **protect the Cuban revolution**.
2. A communist controlled Cuba would provide the USSR with a springboard to **spread communism** to underdeveloped countries in Latin America.
3. They could claim that Russia wanted to protect a small state against a superpower. It would **strengthen the Russian position in the 3rd World.**
4. At the time the US had 100 intercontinental ballistic missiles (ICBM) and 1,700 intercontinental bombers. The USSR had only 50 ICBM and 150 bombers. An intermediate range missile in Cuba would reach major cities in the US and compensate for the lack of ICBM. In practical terms Khrushchev would **reduce the missile gap** with intermediate missiles in Cuba which would save an enormous amount of money for the USSR and put his country in a better strategic position. The alternative, an expensive build-up of Russian ICBM missiles was very expensive.
5. It would put the USSR in a **bargaining position** towards the US. "Quid pro quo" i.e. "something in return" was typical of the Cold War. Some kind of solution to the Berlin problem was one possible option.
6. The US had nuclear missiles in **Turkey**. Khrushchev wrote in his memoirs: *"The Americans had surrounded our country with missile bases and threatened us with nuclear weapons, and now they would learn just what it feels like to have enemy missiles pointing at you".(ref missile crisis)*
7. To show toughness to Khrushchev's critics in China and in the USSR.

**What were the results?**

1. Account for the **missile crisis** (but notice that it is not a question that is specifically asking for the story of the missiles crisis). It is possible to write a lot here.
2. Account for how the crisis was **resolved** (US pledge not to invade, dismantling of missiles in Cuba and Turkey)
3. In a short term perspective it led to a relaxation of great power relations.
4. **The Test Ban Treaty**
5. The setting up of the **Hot Line**.
6. It contributed to some extent to the **fall of Khrushchev** in 1964.
7. The existence of a communist state in the Caribbean had a **profound effect on US policies in the area**. The Cuban example should not be followed in Latin America. The embargo was not lifted.
8. In a long-term perspective the USSR decided to **close the missile gap**. It resulted in an extremely costly nuclear build up in the USSR which probably affected the Russian economy to a very large extent. The missile gap was closed around 1970.

**Conclusion:** Summarise the main point of the essay. Emphasise that the world has never been as close to a nuclear war as in 1962 during this crisis. Emphasise also that one result of this crisis was a Soviet nuclear build up for the rest of the 60s (It is often ignored).

Essay Title: **9. Why has Cuba been an important country in Cold War history?**

Introductory points:

Conclusion:

9. **Why has Cuba been an important country in Cold War history?** *(go through this question chronologically and analyse Cuban policies why the Americans have found it so difficult to accept a communist state in the Caribbean.. It is actually interesting to notice that the trade embargo is still in effect years after the end of the Cold War).*

1. This is a Cold War account. So why not start by explaining the Monroe Doctrine and the views of the OAS and how the Americans perceived Latin America and Central America with the Caribbean as a **US sphere of influence**. It will at least explain why the Americans were not prepared to accept a left wing regime close to the US.
2. Account for the advent of **Castro's regime** and his left wing policies.
3. Explain how the Americans responded with **sabotage, a trade embargo and the Bay of Pigs.**
4. Explain how Fidel turned to the USSR and allowed a Russian militarization of Cuba leading to the **nuclear installations. To Khrushchev** and the USSR Cuba was of major importance, both internationally and also for domestic reasons. By giving Cuba missiles Khrushchev would close the missile gap, protect the Cuban revolution and show toughness to his ctitics.
5. Write about the missiles **crisis**. (Don't overwrite it)
6. The outcome resulted in a communist state in the Caribbean which was not accepted by the US. The embargo is still not lifted even though the fall of communism and the end of the Cold War are years back.
7. Some support was given to attempts to spread the revolution to other countries in the area in the 1960s especially, and to create "**many Vietnams". Che Guevara in Bolivia** is one example.
8. In the 1970s Cuba involved herself in the new battlefield of the Cold War, Africa. Cuba sent troops to both **Angola and Ethiopia.** The development in Africa had a major impact in the US and is one important factor to the end of détente and the beginning of the Second Cold War.
9. Cuba didn't play any major role in Nicaragua but the government still wanted Cuban advisers to return to Cuba, to avoid a US invasion. This is an indication that Cuba was still seen as a very important country which affected US policies in the region.

**Conclusion:** It is perhaps difficult to fully understand the importance of Cuba in the Cold War. It is however clear that it has been of major importance. Our answer to why it has been so important is that it is a combination of how serious the missile crisis actually was and the fact that it is an American country that has turned to communism, close to the US border. It is in a US sphere of influence. There was also a risk that Cuba could have inspired other Latin America countries to turn to communism. Fidel has also been quite provocative to the US by sending Cuban troops to African countries.

**Essay Title: 10. Why was Germany a centre of Cold War problems in the years 1945-61**

Introductory points:

Conclusion:

**10. Why was Germany a centre of Cold War problems in the years 1945-61?** *(Again a list question which you can go through chronologically)*

1. Write about how the defeat of Germany in 1945 resulted in this leading country not existing politically and militarily when the war ended. There was an enormous **power vacuum** in the centre of Europe and this is the main explanation for the Cold War in Europe. Who was going to dominate the strongest economical power in Europe?
2. **At the Yalta Conference** (and a number of different war-time conferences) it was decided to create **zones of occupation** and that there should be a Western zone in **Berlin,**. a capitalist island within the Eastern zone. Explain the significance of the **Allied Control Council** and its veto power.
3. Continue with the **Potsdam** meeting where an agreement was made about the future status of German and the disagreement about the **reparation** payments and how it was solved.
4. It is now possible to discuss how problems occurred as the occupational forces had developed **different aims**. The Western powers wanted to build up Germany economically as a bulwark against communism in Europe. They were also prepared to accept a rebirth of German political life. Stalin was more defensive and feared a rebirth of Germany. Consequently he opposed the policies outlined by the Americans in Byrnes's Stuttgart speech from 1946. It is also possible to write a few words about how the Allied Control Council didn't work due to the veto power of each occupational state and the creation of Bizonia in 1947.
5. Explain how the currency reform led to the **Berlin airlift** in 1948-49.
6. The Berlin airlift showed that no real co-operation was possible and as a result the independent **German states** were proclaimed in 1949.
7. Tension during the crisis led to the formation of **NATO**. Germany did not become a member in 1949, but should be protected by NATO forces in case of a conflict.
8. In 1953 there was a revolt in East Germany against Soviet control, which was crushed by the Red Army.
9. The question of a German membership of NATO was brought up by the Americans during the Korean War and was opposed both by the USSR and France. It was finally solved in **1955** when Germany became a **full member**. German troops were allowed again.
10. Explain the importance of the Marshall Plan to West Germany and how this created problems especially in Berlin. There was a revolt in Berlin against Soviet control in 1953. Write about how approximately 200,000 **East Germans fled the country** every year in the 1950s and how this must have affected the economy of the East.
11. Write about how Khrushchev tried to solve this with his **first Berlin ultimatum in 1958**
12. Write about how Khrushchev again made attempts to solve the Berlin problem at the summits in 1960 and 61.
13. When no solution was reached, the **Berlin Wall was erected in 1961**.
14. You could include some **historiography** here. To an orthodox historian Germany is a typical example of the aggressiveness of the communists. Germany was not in any sense a Russian sphere of influence but Stalin wanted to take control. To a revisionist Germany is a typical example of "dollar imperialism" because the country was dependent on US capital for its reconstruction. This dependence led to political control.

**Conclusion:** The most important reason why Germany was so important is its economic potential in combination with there being a power vacuum after the war. The Berlin solution from Yalta/Potsdam is also important because this island within the Eastern zone resulted in so much tension later, creating the Berlin airlift and the problems with the refugees.

Essay Title: **11. "The Asian development of the Cold War was far more dangerous than European development". With reference to events from the period 1945-61, how far do you agree?**

Introductory points:

1st main part:

2nd main part:

Conclusion:

**11. "The Asian development of the Cold War was far more dangerous than European development". With reference to events from the period 1945-61, how far do you agree?**
*("How far do you agree" means that you have to write one part where you show how the development in Asia was dangerous and a second part showing how the development in Europe was dangerous, and then you conclude and show if you agree)*

**The Asian development was dangerous in the Cold War:**
1. It can be argued that the situation in Asia was more unstable than in Europe. **The Chinese Civil War** restarted in 1945 and ended in 1949. In total some 4-5 million soldiers were fighting in this war. On the other hand there was no major foreign military involvement. But this was not the only armed conflict in the area during this period **The Korean war 1950-53, the Indochina war started in 1946, the islands between mainland China and Taiwan were bombed in 1954-55, China occupied Tibet in 1951.** The situation in Europe, except for a few clashes, was more stable.
2. The Korean War was a very dangerous conflict. There were two critical moments in this war. In late 1950 the UN forces were close to the Yalu river, the border to China. The fact that 300,000 **Chinese soldiers attacked UN forces** at that moment was a major crisis. The second crisis was when MacArthur threatened China with a **nuclear attack** and wanted to widen the war. He was dismissed in April 1951 by President Truman. An attack on China may have triggered a major conflict or perhaps a World War III. MacArthur was able to put a lot of pressure on Truman and told the Congress after his dismissal that he had not been permitted (by Truman) to destroy the enemy. When Truman finally dismissed MacArthur he said it was the most difficult decision he made during his political life. Truman had dropped the A-bomb in 1945.
3. There were two major crises in Sino-American relation in the mid 50s. There are some small **islands in the Taiwan Straits** between Taiwan and China, called Quemoy and Matsu islands. In 1954 the leader in Taiwan, threatened China with a "holy war". China responded with an artillery bombardment in late 1954 and early 55. The crisis led to a renewed US pledge to defend Taiwan. When the Chinese conquered another island, Tachen, the US Congress gave Eisenhower a resolution allowing the President to take whatever actions he found necessary. Eisenhower now announced that aggression from the communists would be met by nuclear arms. In 1958 there were new bombardments and again the **US threatened with the use of nuclear arms.**
4. In **Indochina there was a war** between the Viet Minh and France. Between 1946-54 110,000 French soldiers were killed. It is difficult to estimate Viet Minh casualties, but it was around 300,000.

The development in Europe was dangerous:

1. There were two **crises over Berlin** which were very tense. When the Russians cut off all the land routes to Berlin in 1948, both sides mobilised. It was a critical moment. When the Berlin Wall was erected in 1961 it was a similar situation with troops from both sides facing each other. But it did not lead to an armed conflict between the US and the USSR.
2. The **Hungarian uprising** was the most violent crisis in Europe between 1945-61. 30,000 Hungarians and 7,000 Russian troops were killed in the uprising. 200,000 Hungarians fled their country. But the US did not try to challenge Soviet authority.
3. The prospect of electoral victories to the communists in countries like Italy and France was seen as a major danger. Western Europe was considered as very important to the "free world".

**Conclusion:** Europe was not without conflicts but the situation in Asia was probably more dangerous.

Essay Title: **12. "It is unjustified to see Khrushchev as a Cold Warrior". Do you agree?**

Introductory points:

1st main part:

2nd main part:

Conclusion:

**12. "It is unjustified to see Khrushchev as a Cold Warrior". Do you agree?** *(Write one part where you argue that it was unjustified and a second part showing that he deserves to be called a Cold warrior).*

**Yes it is unjustified:**
1. He took many initiatives like accepting the independence of **Austria in 1955, the visit to Yugoslavia in 1955 accepting "national communism", withdrawal of troops from Finland in 1955, dissolving Cominform in 1956**, showing signs of détente.
1. In the **Secret Speech** from 1956 Khrushchev showed political braveness by challenging orthodox Stalinism in several ways. He indicated that there could be a liberalisation of policies towards the satellites. He also showed that he believed in **peaceful co-existence** with the capitalist West which was a clear rejection of orthodox Marxist-Leninism.
2. He accepted a form of liberalisation in **Poland** in 1956.
3. Hungary will be the main point in the "no-part" below. But you can argue that the Hungarians went too far demanding a multi-party system and to leave the Warsaw pact. It would lead to a domino reaction in Eastern Europe and left Khrushchev with no alternative if he wanted to survive politically. One can understand why he acted but not to justify all the violence.
4. He never really pressed his point over Berlin. After all, the erection of the Berlin Wall did not lead to a war over Berlin.
5. **The Cuban crisis** is probably the second point against him. He can be defended by arguing that he wanted to defend the Cuban revolution, by doing only the same thing that the Americans had done in Turkey. It was Khrushchev who gave in and accepted a portrayal as a "loser", to preserve the peace.
6. It is worth emphasising that he didn't allow the transfer of Soviet **nuclear technology to Mao** in China. The reason was probably that he didn't trust Mao to handle these weapons with care. Khrushchev had to pay a high political price for this refusal as it is one of the main reasons for the Sino-Soviet split.
7. He made substantial **reductions to the Russian Red Army** for which he paid a high political price
8. After the missiles crisis in 1962 the USSR signed both the **Test Ban Treaty** and accepted setting up a **Hot Line**, to improve communications.

**No he deserves the reputation as a Cold Warrior:**
1. We cannot ignore the fact that he was responsible for crushing the **Hungarian uprising** which led to the killing of 30,000 Hungarians. Nagy was also executed. If we compare him to Gorbachev, he allowed a peaceful transformation of the satellites and respected the will of the populations in the satellites. Khrushchev did not.
2. Khrushchev was much more adventurous. In 1955 the Czechs made an **arms deal with Egypt.** This couldn't be done without an approval from Moscow. Khrushchev was the first leader to arm allies that were not bordering the Soviet Union.
3. In the late 1950s Khrushchev announced that he believed that the ultimate victory of communism would be achieved through *"national-liberation wars"* in the Third World and that he would support such wars wholeheartedly and without reservation. It was a dangerous escalation of the Cold War. It would lead to engagements in Vietnam and Cuba.
4. Khrushchev was the aggressor over **Berlin** in 1958 with his first ultimatum. He issued a second ultimatum in Vienna 1961, and was behind the erection of the Berlin Wall later in 1961.
5. The world has never been as close to a nuclear war as during the **Cuban Missile crisis** in 1962. He should have been aware that he was putting Kennedy in an impossible situation by placing missiles in Cuba and he must therefore be held partly responsible for this crisis.

**Conclusion:** It is possible to argue the he was a typical representative for this time: He played both the détente and confrontation games.

# Part III: Détente

**Overview**

The third period that will be outlined in his guide is a period of **détente** which took place after tthe **Vietnam War** in the 1970s and ended with the Soviet invasion of **Afghanistan** in 1979. There are some historians who argue that this relaxation of strain started after the Cuban missile crisis. Others argue that it started when the Americans realised that the **economic and military consequences of the Vietnam War** started to threaten the US and when the Russians were finally able to close the **missile gap** and start to discuss with the US from a position of strength. A third factor which affected superpower relations was the development in **China**. In 1969 there were armed conflicts between Chinese and Soviet forces in the Ussuri river at the border between the two communist states. China soon announced an end to isolation during the Cultural Revolution and invited Richard Nixon to Beijing in 1972. The USSR feared a close co-operation between the US and China and had to reconsider her position in the Cold War triangle.

It was Nixon and his National Security Adviser Henry Kissinger who outlined the US motives for **détente**. By accepting nuclear parity with the Soviets and Soviet spheres of influences, the Russians would support a peace settlement in Vietnam, arms control and co-operate with the US to maintain stability in the Third World. To accept Soviet parity was an acceptance of a **balance of power**. Access to Western technology and investments should also promote Soviet co-operation, hence the idea of **"linkage"**.

There are several important agreements from this period showing a new atmosphere of co-operation. In 1968 **the Nuclear Non-Proliferation Treaty** was signed to prevent a proliferation of nuclear weapons. The Strategic Arms Limitation Talks or **SALT** started in 1969 and were finished in 1972 resulting in a **freeze** on ICBM (intercontinental ballistic missiles), SLBM (submarine launched ballistic missiles) and ICB (intercontinental bombers). It was however only a freeze and no reduction. An **Anti-Ballistic Missile Treaty** (ABM) was also signed limiting the development of such systems. SALT II was signed in 1979 but the agreement was never ratified by US Congress. There were many other treaties signed during this period as a result of a better understanding. In 1973 there was a ceasefire in **Vietnam**. In 1975 **The Helsinki Final Act** was signed where the 1945 borders in Europe were recognised as inviolable, pleasing the Soviets. The Western powers were pleased as the agreement stipulated that human rights were universal and that there should be free exchange of ideas and people across Europe.

It is normally considered that this period of détente came to an end in 1979 when the USSR invaded **Afghanistan**, probably the worst mistake made by the Soviets during the Cold War. The US post-Vietnam policies of reluctance to intervene in conflicts abroad enabled the USSR to extend their positions especially in the Third World. Cuban soldiers supported by the USSR were fighting in **Angola and Ethiopia** in the late 70s. The seeds of the end of détente can be found in this period. It would result in a "Second Cold War" and it would bring **Ronald Reagan to power.**

**The Indo-China and Vietnam Wars 1946-75.**

> The French and the American involvement in armed conflicts in Indo-China lasted from 1946-1973. In this text these two conflicts will be referred to as **the Indo-China War** and **the Vietnam War** (sometimes called the second Indo-China war). You should be able to put these conflicts in an appropriate Cold War context as a part of your Cold War preparation. The focus of this text will be the international implications and not the wars, even though the main events will be outlined. The most important part of this conflict, from an international and Cold War perspective is the period after President Johnson's escalation after 1965.,This led to new positions in the Cold War triangle and is the reason why you find this conflict in the "détente period" in the guide.

**The Indo-China War 1946-54.**

In 1943 Churchill and Roosevelt had signed the **Cairo Declaration** where *"Japan will also be expelled from all other territories which she has taken by violence and greed"* during the war. At **Potsdam** it was confirmed that *"the terms of the Cairo Declaration shall be carried out"* and that these territories should be *"free and independent"*. *(ref. see the Potsdam meeting in 1945)*

French Indo-China (Vietnam, Cambodia and Laos) had been a part of the French Empire since the late 19th century. After the **Potsdam** meeting and the sudden Japanese surrender in 1945, it was decided that **Britain should re-occupy the South and Jiang's Nationalists the North**, until the French were able to return. Support had been given to France to return and take control.

- France and the post war government led by **General De Gaulle** had no intention of embarking on a de-colonisation process. **A restoration of France and national prestige after the humiliation during the German occupation** in combination with a fear of a **"domino-reaction" within her colonies** made the French determined to re-impose control.
- During the war Roosevelt had been inconsistent about the future of Indo-China. Finally in 1945 the US decided to support the return of the French. France was seen as **an important ally in Europe**.

The League for the Independence of Vietnam (**Viet Minh**) had been formed in 1941 to oppose Japanese occupation. It was composed of different groups but led and controlled by the communists under Ho Chi Minh. Since 1943 they had been fighting the Japanese and liberated parts of the country. **The Chinese Nationalists didn't take firm political control** in the North due to problems in China and in September 1945 Ho could proclaim the foundation of the **Democratic Republic of Vietnam (DRV) in Hanoi**. The French government was not prepared to accept his regime and in 1946 a full scale war started between the Viet Minh and the French – **the Indo-China War** (1946-54).

Ho Chi Minh

**Course of events:**

- In November 1946 the French attacked Hanoi and Haipong and 6,000 people were killed.
- Ho and the Viet Minh now started a guerrilla war. The size of the Viet Minh in late 1946 was around 80 000 men, poorly equipped compared to the French army which was made up of 115,000 men. The Viet Minh were brilliantly led by General Vo Nguyen Giap. The Indo-China War was initially a war of national liberation from colonialism.
- In 1949 the French offered a limited independence, partly due to pressure from the US. **Bao Dai should** remain in power. It was rejected by the Viet Minh as Dai was seen as a **French puppet**. He had previously been a puppet to the Japanese.
- The Viet Minh forces were able to fight a successful war using guerrilla tactics. In 1950 the French suffered a major defeat at Cao Bang. It was in 1949 and 1950 that the **international implications** became more important. In October 1949 Mao came to power in China. In June 1950, just after the outbreak of the Korean War, Chinese military advisers and weapons were sent to Vietnam. In 1950 79 Chinese officers and military advisers arrived to the North and China delivered 14,000 small arms, 1,700 machine guns and 150 artillery pieces.
- It was also in 1950, when the Korean War started, that Truman and the Americans started to support the French in the Indo-China War. From 1950 to 1954 the Americans gradually increased their economic support to the French and in 1954, when France pulled out, the **Americans were paying** more than 70 % of France's cost for the war.
- American pressure led to more aggressive French military plans, the so-called Navarre Plan in 1954. But the escalation also led to **domestic opposition in France**. 110,000 Frenchmen were killed in the conflict and it finally convinced the French government that it had to withdraw.
- The Viet Minh victory was accomplished when the French were defeated at the battle of **Dien Bien Phu** in May 1954, after a 50-day siege. In June the French government fell from power and the new Prime Minister, Mendéz-France, pledged to end the war within thirty days or resign.

**How did the Cold War affect the Great Powers at Geneva?**

- The US wanted to exclude France from Vietnam to be able to **fight the communists** more effectively. Indo-China was at this time seen as a **cornerstone** in the struggle against communism in Asia. The US didn't sign the **Final Declaration** because it would be seen as recognition of Red China. When France left Vietnam after 1954, she had received more money from the US than from Europe through the Marshall Plan.
- The USSR also wanted to end the conflict. The new leadership after Stalin wanted to **relax the tension**. In 1954 the Americans wanted to bring West Germany into **NATO** and the Soviets hoped that France would oppose this. In 1955 when Ho visited both Moscow and Beijing he was promised limited economic help but no military support. The North had to limit their struggle to unify the country in 'diplomatic struggle'.
- China wanted Western powers out of Indo-China. She feared an **American intervention,** a new Korea.
- The peace conference in Geneva ended the Indo-China War in July. At the Geneva conference the UK, USSR, France, the US, China and the states of Indo-China participated. It was agreed that:

    1. Laos and Cambodia should gain independence.
    2. There should be a ceasefire in Vietnam and the country was **temporarily divided** at the 17$^{th}$ parallel pending the general elections which will bring about the unification of Vietnam'. Ho's regime in the North was recognised.
    3. General elections should be held in July 1956 and then the country should be unified.

- During the conference Ngo Diem, backed by the US, became Prime Minister in the South. He had every reason to prevent the elections as Ho was expected to win. Diem also decided to do this, backed by the Americans.

- In 1954 the **SEATO** (the South East Treaty Organisation) was set up by the US, France, Britain, Australia, New Zealand, the Philippines, Thailand and Pakistan, in an attempt to prevent the spread of communism in South East Asia.

The Indo-China War had been transformed from a war of de-colonisation to a part of the Cold War.

**The Vietnam War.**

- **Diem**, with the support of the US, cancelled the elections that should have been held in 1956.
- Diem was a Catholic leader in a country where 75 % of the population were Buddhists. His regime is normally described as corrupt and he lacked support from the population. The reasons for this may have been his reluctance to carry out a genuine land reform and that he was seen by many as an American puppet when he arrived from Paris in 1954. US support was crucial: they soon gave Diem $ 300 million in assistance.
- The period after Geneva is normally described as relatively calm partly due to the fact that Ho consolidated his regime in the North, implementing a land reform. One million refugees fled to the South and there was no time for organising armed rebellion in the South.
- With the **Sino Soviet split** in the late 50s the situation changed. Both China and the USSR wanted to be the leading communist state and influence in Vietnam became important to both of them. In 1959 both China and the USSR decided to **support an armed national liberation struggle** in Vietnam and the North now pledged themselves to a reunification by armed struggle. Khrushchev announced in 1960 that the ultimate victory of communism would be achieved through **"wars of liberation"** in the Third World, and promised help to Vietnam.
- In 1959 the North decided to unify the country by military means if necessary. In **1960** the guerrillas in the South, **Viet Cong, intensified their activities**. In 1961 alone, 4,000 civil servants were killed by guerrillas in the South. In the same year different groups formed the National Liberation Front (NLF). It was the political arm of the Viet Cong. When Kennedy came to power in early 1961 he inherited 400 military advisers from the Eisenhower administration. When he was assassinated in November 1963, there were 16,000 advisers, but still no real combat troops, except for pilots flying combat missions. Kennedy now had an opportunity to show his "flexible response" policy, to fight communism with a wide range of weapons. Threatening to use nuclear weapons in the Vietnamese conflict was no use. Military advisers, economic support to the regime and a programme of building "strategic hamlets" where peasants were supposed to be protected from guerrillas were parts of this policy. The guerrillas however intensified their activities and attacked government buildings and officials. Diem's regime suffered from a lack of genuine support and in 1960 the US ambassador wondered if it was not time to support an 'alternative leadership in Saigon'.
- In November 1963 **Diem was murdered** during a military coup. It would now be military generals who would lead the South, totally dependent on the US. The Americans realised that the absence of a leader in the South with support from the population was one major obstacle to establishing an alternative to Ho in the North. But there was no easy solution to this problem in late 1963.
- In August 1964 the US Congress accepted giving the president the right to *"take all necessary steps, including the use of armed force"*[73] to defend South Vietnam. This was a result of a naval incident in the **Gulf of Tonking**. The result was that Johnson could **escalate** the Vietnam conflict without a formal declaration of war, which has to be made by the Congress. there was an absence of public awareness of the significance of the resolution and why America was suddenly engulfed in a major war in Vietnam. It would backfire when US soldiers were killed and no victory was delivered. Many Congressmen preferred this solution in 1964 when it was an election year.

**Lyndon B Johnson**

- In 1965 President Johnson started to escalate the conflict. Vietnam was now without doubt the focus of US Cold War policies. In the meantime the Sino Soviet dispute was more tense than ever. But both powers supported the North. After Khrushchev was overthrown in 1964, one of the new leaders, Kosygin, went to Hanoi and made the Soviet support public in 1965. China also gave massive economic and military aid. Troops from the North were trained in China and 50,000 road and rail construction forces from the Chinese army were sent to the North. **This aid was absolutely necessary for the North to fight this war.**
- Combat troops were sent to Vietnam in 1965. Now the Americans had 180,000 US troops in the country. In 1968 the number had increased to 540,000 men. In 1965 the US started to air bomb the North.
- In 1964 Viet Minh forces started to fight against the Viet Cong in the South.
- **The Tet (lunar new year) offensive** in January 1968 was a **major turning point** which convinced many Americans that the war could not be won. In spite of an enormous superiority in resources and equipment, the guerrillas suddenly attacked Saigon and a hundred other cities. The presidential palace in Saigon, the US Embassy, airports and radio stations were all under attack. The NLF had to take high casualties and 50,000 NLFs were killed, but the psychological impact of the offensive was of major importance.
- The anti-war movement in the US grew in strength. Robert Kennedy, the brother of slain president and a Democrat, announced that he was going to challenge the Democrat Johnson. Johnson now had to fight for his nomination within his own party. In March 1968 Johnson announced that he would not stand for re-election. His social reform programme "Great Society" had been undermined by the costs of the war and in 1968 300 US soldiers were killed every week and there was no prospect of victory.
- In 1968 Richard M **Nixon** was elected US President. He introduced a new policy of **Vietnamisation.** The South Vietnamese army should gradually increase its involvement while the Americans should gradually withdraw. Financial aid should continue. This policy was confirmed in the **Nixon Doctrine** from 1969. Peace talks now started in Paris and the aim was *'peace with honour'*.
- **The US wanted to end the Vietnam War.** To be able to do that they needed support from both the USSR and China. The US desire to end the Vietnam War with honour and to restore a strong economy, made them genuinely try to promote détente. There had not been any comparable and genuine attempt made by the Americans since 1945. The US now offered the Soviets a deal, the **idea of linkage**: The US would recognise the USSR's strategic parity and would not interfere in the Soviet empire and would allow the Soviets to get access to Western technology if the USSR helped the Americans out if Vietnam, an **end of the idea of "roll-back"**
- **China had gone through the Cultural Revolution and was isolated**. The relation with the USSR was more tense than ever and the Americans were fighting a war south of her border. The Warsaw Pact invasion of Czechoslovakia in 1968 and armed border disputes with the

Soviets in 1969 alarmed the Chinese. An understanding between the Soviets and the Americans was the worst possible scenario. The rapprochement with the US convinced the Chinese that they did not have to fear a US-Soviet alliance against China and in 1971 China was finally accepted in the UN, replacing Taiwan.
- The Sino Soviet dispute also affected the USSR. The border disputes in 1969 had the effect of an 'electric shock' in Moscow". **The Soviets feared an invasion of millions of Chinese** radicals. In the early 70s the Soviets had finally been able to close the missile gap and had a strong position versus the US and could also avoid a further nuclear build-up. An understanding with the US was more possible than ever. The Soviets feared **an understanding between the US and China.**
- In order to put pressure on the North and to cut off supplies, the war was expanded to **Cambodia in 1969** with air bombardment and later an invasion.
- It was estimated that 400 universities and colleges were temporarily closed down in 1970 due to student strikes.
- In 1971 US and South Vietnamese forces invaded Laos to support the government against the guerrillas.
- While peace talks dragged on, there was intense air bombing of the North. In 1971 **Nixon** announced that he **would visit China** the next year.
- On January 27 **1973 a peace agreement** was finally signed and a cease-fire should come into effect the next day. The **US forces should be withdrawn** and both sides committed themselves to reunification by peaceful means. Before leaving, the Americans supplied the regime in the South with everything they needed to continue the war. As an example the South now acquired the world's fourth biggest air force.
- After the Americans left, the conflict soon restarted but now as a civil war. **In 1975 the North conquered the South** and the conflict was finally brought to an end.

---

As explained earlier, it is not the war that you are supposed to write about. The aim is to analyse the Vietnam War as a part of the Cold War i.e. to demonstrate the international implications.

---

The 1970s resulted in several arms limitation agreements and, which was more sensational, a US-Chinese rapprochement.

**How did the Vietnam War affect the 1970s?**

- The war had been a **'bleeding wound'** for the US. It affected her **economy** and her **prestige abroad**. It is the main explanation for why the US turned to **détente in the 1970s**. It also led to a **reluctance to be involved in armed conflicts in the Third World** on the part of the US. This is shown in the **Nixon Doctrine** from 1969 where Nixon announced that the US should mainly support allies in the Third World and not do the fighting in the future. The idea of "**linkage**" also brought an end to the idea of a '**roll back**' of communism.
- US determination to get out of Vietnam was one reason behind the **rapprochement with China** in the early 1970s. There were other reasons behind this rapprochement like Chinese isolation during the Cultural Revolution and the Sino-Soviet dispute, but the Vietnam War was very significant.
- With a Chinese-US understanding, the USSR feared that if they pushed the US too hard, it would drive the US and China closer together. This was one, but not the only, reason for the **USSR finally supporting détente** in the 70s.
- There are historians who argue that the US reluctance to get involved in armed conflicts in the Third World later in the 70s would enable the Soviets to follow a more aggressive policy there. Soviet and Cuban support in the Civil wars in **Angola and Ethiopia** are two examples. A third example is the Soviet invasion of **Afghanistan** in 1979 which led to "the Second Cold War" during the **Reagan** era.

In conclusion it can be said that even though the war had soured relations between the blocs for decades, the Vietnam War actually provided an opportunity for détente in the 70s. But it must also be emphasised that this was not the only reason for détente. It had deeper roots which can be seen in the description of the Cold War triangle above. More about this later.

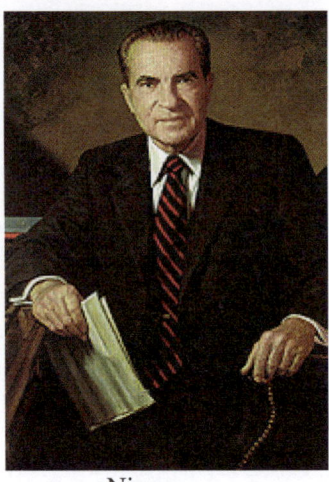

Brezhnev Nixon Mao

**Why was there a period of détente in the late 60s and 70s?**

- The Soviet Union had finally **closed the missile gap.** Now both the US and the USSR had achieved MAD, Mutual Assured Destruction. Brezhnev told the Central Committee in 1972: *"The correlation of forces between the USSR and the US…is now more favourable than ever before."*[74] The USSR was now anxious to reduce her costs and of course also **reduce the risk of war**. This was especially important because the growth of the Soviet **economy was stagnating**. Gross National Product had grown by 5 % annually between 1966 and 1970. In 1971-75 it was 3.6 %. In the late 70s it was only 22 %. The USSR wanted to avoid a continuation of a development of sophisticated and expensive technological nuclear weapons. Nixon's policy of linkage offered opportunities for an increase in **East-West trade** and Western **technology**. Finally the USSR was alarmed by the **Sino-Soviet split** and the border clashes in 1969.
- The US wanted out of **Vietnam**. The war had eroded the **US economy** and its prestige and threatened her status globally. Arms agreements would not only **reduce the risk of war**, but also bring down the cost of arms development. The US economy had suffered from the Vietnam War and was in recession from 1973. There was also a very strong anti-war movement in the US and Nixon needed an understanding with both the USSR and China to get out of the war. The technological development of new weapons was not only costly but also dangerous. Kissinger believed in an explosion of technology and the number of nuclear weapons, if no arms deal was made.
- China wanted to end her isolation after the Cultural Revolution.

**Examples of détente 1968-79.**

- **1968 The Non-Proliferation of Nuclear Weapons Treaty.** This early agreement was signed by the US, USSR and Britain and the aim was to prevent the transfer of nuclear technology to other countries. The two other nuclear countries in the world, China and France, refused to sign.
- **1969 SALT (Strategic Arms Limitation Talks)** negotiations between the US and USSR started.

> "**Strategic nuclear arms**" means long range nuclear weapons and can be used to bomb cities. A missile can be launched from a submarine (SLBM) or from another continent (ICBM)
> "**Tactical nuclear weapons**" are short range and can be used against enemy forces.

- **1971 Nuclear Accidents Agreement** between the US and USSR was an agreement where both powers promised to increase safeguards against the unauthorised firing of nuclear weapons and to notify the other part if an incident occurred.
- **1972 SALT 1** signed by Nixon and Brezhnev. It was an important agreement resulting in a freeze on strategic nuclear weapons. It comprised two parts:
    - **The Interim Agreement on Offensive Arms.** This agreement resulted in a maximum level of ICBM and SLBM but did not place any limits on long-range strategic bombers (ICB). This five year freeze on levels of ICBM and SLBM was no reduction of the number of weapons but a successful agreement to prevent a further escalation of the arms development. Nothing was said about the number of long-range bombers and the development of MIRVs (multiple independently targeted re-entry vehicles), nuclear weapons with many warheads, where each was capable of being directed to a specific target.
    - **The Anti Ballistic Missile (ABM) Treaty.** ABM is a system with weapons that are able to shoot down enemy missiles. It was now decided that each side should only have two systems with no more than 100 missile launchers each. The idea of limiting this protection was that if one side had a strong protection it might encourage this state to risk a nuclear war.

Even though SALT I was only a freeze and no decisions were taken about MIRVs and ICBs, the agreement was an important change in Cold War relations and would result in a continuing process of détente.
The SALT agreement was a recognition of Soviet equality in nuclear weapons. It was also a recognition that a nuclear war would mean the destruction of both, hence a war must be avoided at any cost. This was referred to as **Mutual Assured Destruction**. This was the idea behind the terror balance: fear of nuclear destruction would lead to peace.

- **1972 The Basic Principles of Relations between the USSR and the US.** This was a formal declaration that both states were committed to peaceful co-existence.
- **1973 The Prevention of Nuclear War Agreement** provided for consultation between the two powers in times of crisis.
- **1975 the Helsinki Agreement** was signed by all European governments (except for Albania) and the US and Canada. The agreement was a formal recognition of the frontiers in Europe. The main points were:

1. Respect for sovereignty;
2. Renunciation of the use of force for settling disputes;
3. Peaceful settlement of disputes
4. Non-intervention in internal affairs;
5. Respect for human rights;
6. Territorial integrity of states; and,
7. The inviolability of frontiers.

With this agreement all post war frontiers in Europe were accepted. The Soviets were pleased because it was an acceptance of the division of Germany and the Soviet sphere of influence. The signatories also agreed to respect human rights i.e. the right to travel and freedom of speech. This was considered to be an important achievement by the Western powers.

- **1979 The SALT II agreement.** This agreement limited the number of ICBMs and SLBM to 2,400 each and included a ceiling on the number of MIRVs. The two powers also promised to notify each other on tests. The treaty was signed but never ratified (approved) by the US Congress, mainly due to the Soviet invasion of Afghanistan, but both sides kept the agreement until 1986.
- What is also important to keep in mind is that there were regular **US-Soviet summits** throughout the 1970s which promoted a better understanding:
1. Moscow 1972: Brezhnev-Nixon
2. Washington 1973: Brezhnev-Nixon
3. Moscow 1974: Brezhnev-Nixon
4. Vladivostok 1974: Brezhnev-Ford
5. Vienna 1979: Brezhnev-Carter

**Ostpolitik.**

Another development which took place in the centre of Europe in the 1970s was an important part of the détente process: **Willy Brandt's Ostpolitik**. West Germany's relation to East Germany had been expressed by Konrad Adenhauer, Chancellor from 1949-63, in the **Hallstein Doctrine** from 1955. West Germany was not prepared to have any diplomatic relations with any state who recognised the East German state. West Germany also refused to recognise its frontier with Poland and Czechoslovakia from 1945. The West German state had been established after the Berlin blockade and was a result of US support. Consequently she was a reliable ally of the US.

Brandt and his adviser Bahr were forming a new foreign policy. The idea was to overcome the **division of Germany and ease the tension in Central Europe**, rather than fight in the front line with the US in the Cold War. Better relations were needed with the USSR. Bahr said: *"The German question can only be solved with the USSR not against it...the preconditions for reunification are only to be created with the USSR."*[75] In 1966 Brandt was appointed Foreign Minister in a coalition with the Christian Democrats. In 1967 diplomatic relations were established with Romania, a rejection of the Hallstein Doctrine. In 1969 the Social Democrats (SPD) won the elections and formed a government with the liberals (FDP) with Brandt as Chancellor. It was now time for change. The US wanted to get out of Vietnam and West Germany wanted a normalisation with its neighbours in the East, to reduce the tension in Central Europe and the get better relations with "the Eastern zone". The USSR was the key to both problems.

- **The Moscow Treaty from 1970** between West Germany and the USSR, formally ended World War II and recognised the frontiers and the agreements from the war i.e. that Poland had been moved to the west at the expense of German territories (the Oder-Neisse line) and the division of Germany.
- **In September 1971 the US, USSR, Britain and France** signed an agreement recognising each other's rights to Berlin.
- **The East German-West German Basic Treaty from 1972** was a formal recognition of two German states and the links from West Germany to West Berlin were accepted i.e. no more Berlin Blockade as in 1948. The agreement aimed at increasing commercial, cultural and personal contacts between **'two states within one nation'** as Brandt expressed it.

This process of European détente was further strengthened and confirmed with the signing of **the Helsinki agreement in 1975.**

## The decline of détente.

The ideas of détente and linkage dominated the post Vietnam War development in the 1970s. But there were several events during this period which would bring the New Right, a coalition between Republicans and neo-conservative Democrats, to power in the US. In 1980 Ronald Reagan was elected US president and his new administration took a much tougher stance against the USSR. Détente was now replaced by the Second Cold War.

> If a "Second Cold War" started in 1979/80, we must ask ourselves: when was the "First Cold War"? Well, it must have been from either the Potsdam meeting in 1945 or the declaration of the Truman Doctrine in 1947 to the Missile Crisis in 1962. An alternative to the Missile Crisis as an end to the first period could be the end of the Vietnam war in the early 1970s. That is the "First Cold War". There were signs of détente in the mid 1950s, but these promising signs were not enough to change the overall impression of this period as being coined by superpower rivalry.

### What challenged détente in the 1970s?

### The Middle East

The Middle East with its oil resources had traditionally been dominated by the West. When Truman announced his Truman Doctrine in 1947, he wanted money not only for Greece, but to Turkey as well. But Stalin didn't really challenge Western interests in the Middle East. It would be different with Khrushchev. From 1955, Nasser's regime in the Middle East received military aid from Czechoslovakia and the USSR which increased the tension in the area. The Baghdad Pact was formed in 1955 and was a Western attempt to contain communism from the Middle East. It was the Suez crisis in 1956 which definitely made the Middle East an important area in the Cold War struggle. Even if the US was not involved in the Western attack, her two most important allies in Europe were behind it. The Anglo-French attack discredited Western interests in the region and opened up for Soviet influence. In January 1957 Eisenhower launched his "**Eisenhower Doctrine**" and the US Congress gave him the right to provide economic and military assistance to any Middle Eastern country threatened with armed aggression or internal subversion. As a result of this the US intervened in Lebanon in July 1957. In 1964 a **Soviet Mediterranean fleet** was formed and in 1966 the USSR signed an agreement which gave the Soviets a naval base in Egypt. This was of major strategic importance to the USSR. For the first time they could really counter US activities in the area. In the Six Day War in 1967 Egypt, Syria and Jordan were defeated and humiliated by the Israelis. The USSR now started to give massive military aid to Egypt with a complete air defence system and 20 000 military advisers. The USSR became an ally of several Arab countries. US support for Israel of course angered the Arabs. **The Israel-Arab conflict became very tense after the Six-Day War** when the Israelis occupied the West Bank and conquered Jerusalem. But it was a delicate act for Marxist Leninists to co-operate with Muslim states in the Middle East. Brezhnev said: *"Nasser is highly confused on ideological questions...but...of inestimable value to us."*[76] When the Soviets refused to supply Egypt with even more modern offensive military systems and refused to help the Arabs to recapture territories lost in the Six Day War, Nasser's successor Sadat expelled Soviet military advisers from the country in 1972. This Soviet refusal was due to its concern for the détente process with the US which had started.

In October 1973 Egypt and Syria launched a surprise attack on Israel, the **Yom Kippur War**. The Israelis were taken by surprise while celebrating Yom Kippur, their most important religious festival. The Arab alliance initially made big advances. Both the US and the USSR started with large-scale airlifts with weapons to their allies. The Israelis recovered quickly and launched a large scale counter attack. They invaded Egypt and crossed the Suez Canal and had soon surrounded an entire Egyptian army. The USSR now called for a joint US-Soviet military intervention and threatened to intervene unilaterally if no support was given from the US. Nixon refused and upgraded the alert status of US military forces worldwide. The USSR had to accept a US proposal of a UN peacekeeping force and the Israelis were forced to reluctantly accept a cease fire.

The war was a fiasco for the USSR. Her allies in the region had been defeated and humiliated and it was the US and Henry Kissinger who played a leading role in solving the crisis. In the US many politicians questioned the intentions of the USSR in the détente process. They had foreknowledge about the attack and neither prevented it nor informed the US. Soviet attempts to extend her influence to new areas previously dominated by the West also had **negative effects on the détente process**. Naval bases around the world were of great strategic importance. The Warsaw Pact had more ships and submarines than NATO but NATO could keep twice as many submarines at sea due to better access to bases. In 1972 the USSR lost her most important base in the Mediterranean and in the Third World. The Yom Kippur war had put strains on superpower relations but too much political prestige had already been invested in the détente process from both sides to let it be destroyed by one international crisis. Brezhnev who was most bitter, concluded in December 1973: *"Matters would look quite different were it not for this factor of détente....if the current conflict had flared up in a situation of universal, international tension...it might...endangering world peace."*[77]

### Africa

In the early 1960s Khrushchev had declared that the ultimate victory of communism would be achieved through wars of **national-liberation.** During 1970 the Third Wold went through a period of remarkable turbulence, often rooted indigenous development, regional rivalry but most importantly de-colonisation process. Traditionally the Third World had been dominated by the Western powers but the challenge to this order, once initiated by Khrushchev, would continue and increase. In 1975 the Portuguese colonies **Angola, Mozambique and Guinea-Bissau** were granted independence after a revolution in Portugal in 1974. The USSR was eager to establish close relations with states that could provide the USSR with naval bases. It was of major strategic importance, especially after the loss of Egypt in 1972. In Angola different guerrilla groups had fought for independence since the 1950s. The MPLA (the Movimento Popular de Libertacao de Angola) was supported by the Soviets while the FNLA (Frente Nacional de Libertacao de Angola) and the UNITA (the Iniao Nacional para a Independencia Total de Angola) were supported by the US, China and South Africa. The Civil War started in February 1975. In 1973 the US Congress had passed a bill, the War Powers Act, restricting the President's ability to send troops to foreign countries without a formal declaration of war. The US post-Vietnam era showed a reluctance to be involved in conflicts in the Third World. When the Soviets provided the MPLA in Angola with massive military aid, backed by some 17,000 Cuban soldiers, no equivalent US support could be given and in 1976 the MPLA controlled most of the country. The Cuban forces had turned the tide in Angola. In Ethiopia the regime was supported by the USSR in the war against Somalia in 1977/78 and again the Cubans sent some 17 000 troops. In 1976 Angola concluded a friendship treaty with the USSR and Mozambique followed in 1977. In the late 1970s the Soviets had a long list of states in Africa with a pro Soviet policy: **Angola, Benin, Congo, Ethiopia, Guinea, Guinea-Bissau and Mozambique. Other states had strong links to China**.

### The emergence of the New Right.

This development had a major impact on US policies. The emerging New Right, an alliance between Republicans and conservative Democrats, argued that détente was a 'one-way street' allowing the Soviets to extend their influence and that the détente policy had been exploited by the Soviet leadership. It would lead to Reagan and the Second Cold War in the early 1980s and the development in Africa was one important reason for this new policy. The Nixon and Kissinger perception of linkage had involved the idea that the USSR would support US attempts to make the Third World more stable, not a playground for the Cold War. Brezhnev and the USSR rejected this view and saw Western domination of poorer countries as a form of neo-imperialism which had to be opposed.

In the US President Nixon had been forced to resign in 1974 due to the Watergate scandal. He was replaced by his vice President Gerald Ford. There was no major change in the foreign policy since

Henry Kissinger, Nixon's National Security Adviser, had been appointed Secretary of State in 1973. **The policy of détente rested on a US acceptance of Soviet nuclear parity and to respect the Soviet sphere of influence, hence a balance of power. Soviet support for arms agreement, withdrawal from Vietnam and stability in the Third World would be accomplished**. It was not only the Soviet economy which would benefit from a reduction of nuclear development. A traditional reluctance in the US to increase taxes had resulted in budget deficits during the Vietnam War and increased inflation. Together with competition from the Japanese and West German industries, it resulted in the US facing her first balance of trade deficit in the 20$^{th}$ century in 1971. After the Yom Kippur war the Arab states started to use the oil weapon to put pressure on the Western states over the Israel-Palestinian problem. The increase of oil prices, the Oil crisis, led to an economic recession in the Western world in the mid 1970s. GNP was stagnant, the inflation rate was about 10 % per year and unemployment reached 7,5 %. Between 1970 to 1980, the US share of global economic output went down from around 38% to 25 %. Oil prices quadrupled and the Soviet Union which exported oil, benefited from this. Gerald Ford lost the presidential elections in 1976 to the Democrat Jimmy Carter. **Carter**, a governor from Georgia had a background as an owner of a peanut farm. He was seen as a new fresh alternative, not representing the political establishment linked to the nightmare of the Vietnam War and the Watergate scandal.

**Jimmy Carter**

If Kissinger's détente was linked to a balance of power, Carter's détente should be **linked to *morals***. Carter wanted to bring an end to US support to repressive regimes simply based on the fact that they were anti-communists. In March 1977 he sent his Secretary of State Cyrus Vance, to Moscow with a proposal to drastically reduce the number of ICBMs and MIRVs. His initiative was rejected by the Soviets. Many felt that détente had brought nothing and politicians were divided over a continuation. Negotiation over a SALT II agreement was going on and domestic pressure forced the US delegation to take a tougher stance. Carter's administration reflected the attitudes in the US in the late 1970s. His two most trusted advisers in foreign policy had very different ideas about foreign policy. **Cyrus Vance** wanted to continue the détente policy. An arms agreement would ease tension and enable the US to cut her defence budget, which was needed for economic reasons. **Zbigniew Brzezinsky** had a Polish background and was Carter's National Security Adviser. As a native Pole he did not trust the Russians and believed that only US strength would make the Soviets agreeable. A renewed nuclear arms race could also ruin the Soviet economy which by now showed clear signs of stagnation. Carter was a newcomer, by many seen as an amateur in foreign policy. The development in Africa put pressure on Carter and soon developments in Afghanistan confirmed the suspicions of the New Right.

**Afghanistan**

It was the Soviet invasion of Afghanistan in 1979 which finally brought an end to the process of détente. In 1978 a left-wing Afghan group from the People's Democratic Party of Afghanistan (PDPA) overthrew the regime led by Muhammed Daoud. The new regime, led by Muhamed Tarakki, soon signed a friendship treaty with the USSR. A left wing **reform programme** was introduced including a land reform and emancipating women. These policies **provoked Islamic fundamentalists** and a civil war started. There were also internal problems within the PDPA between two factions, the Khalq and Parcham factions. The civil war escalated in 1979, and so did factional fighting. **In December 1979 the USSR sent 85 000 troops** to Afghanistan in an attempt to establish order and control. The leader of the Parcham faction, Babrak Kamal was installed as President. Again there was widespread resistance against the regime and soon some 100 000 Soviet troops were involved in a war against a highly motivated **Muslim guerrilla**. The guerrilla was provided with funds and weapons by the Americans. It was not until 1988 that Gorbachev announced a gradual withdrawal which was completed in 1989. The civil war continued however and finally brought the Taliban to power.
The US reacted strongly against the invasion. Why?

- Many leading politicians in the US had started to question the détente process and could now argue that this was another example, not only in Africa, where **the Soviets cynically exploited the détente process** to extend their influence to new areas. This put a lot of pressure on President Carter to take strong action.
- In the same year the pro-American Shah in Iran was deposed in a fundamentalist revolution, denouncing American influence. A radical anti-American fundamentalist revolution in the oil-rich Middle East threatened vital American interest. If the USSR extended her influence in the region, it was another threat. **By opposing the Soviets and supporting the guerrilla in Afghanistan, the US saw an opportunity to side with the Muslim world at a critical moment**. Moscow had thrown a lifeline to the US in a critical region.

**To the USSR Afghanistan had far reaching consequences:**

- In the Muslim world, the USSR now suddenly had a **"third front"**. It was now not only capitalists in the west, and China in the east, who were enemies.
- It brought an **end to the détente** process with the Americans and there was a risk that an expensive nuclear development could start again. It is often said that the war converted Carter to supporting the Brzezinski hard line policy. Carter said: *"My opinion of the Russians has changed more drastically in the last week than even the previous two and a half years before that."*[78] Carter now **froze the ratification (approval) of Salt II** (it had been signed in 1979) and placed an **embargo on grain exports** to the USSR and the US decided to **boycott the Olympic Games** in Moscow in 1980. The Persian Gulf was militarised by the US and Carter introduced his **Carter Doctrine**: the Persian Gulf was of vital strategic importance to the US and they would deal directly with an outside force trying to gain control of the region. In 1980 the US also provided **China with military equipment** for the first time. Carter's actions are normally described as a start of the "**Second Cold War**".
- It can be argued that the war in Afghanistan contributed to the election of Ronald Reagan as US president in 1980. Reagan would describe the USSR as an "evil empire".
- The Soviet Union lost influence and support in the Third World and in the Non-Aligned movement.
- It put a lot of **economic pressure on the Soviet economy** which had already suffered from stagnation.
- It affected relations with the satellites and China negatively.
- In the Asian republics within the USSR, there was a large Muslim population. It destabilised this part of the Russian empire. Radical Islamist groups gained support.
- The USSR lost **15,000 soldiers and 37,000 were wounded**. (It has been estimated that 1 million Afghanis died during the war).

- In 1985 Saudi Arabia increased her oil production fourfold which led to a collapse of the oil prices. The USSR lost $19 billions per year which had severe effects on the economy.

A final factor challenging the détente process in the late 1970s was the deployment of Soviet SS-20 missiles. The Soviets started to deploy a new type of intermediate range missiles in the USSR in 1977. They were targeted on Western Europe and China. These missiles were movable, had a longer range compared to the missiles they replaced and were of the MIRV class, consequently a clear improvement. As a response the US and NATO decided to deploy their Cruise and Pershing II missiles in Europe. Cruise missiles flew at low level and were difficult to detect by radar and could be used for surprise attacks. In December 1979 NATO announced that from 1983 there would be 108 Pershings and 464 Tomahawks missiles deployed in Western Europe. The decision alarmed the Soviets as it was seen as a Western attempt to achieve a first strike option against the USSR. It not only alarmed the Soviets, anti nuclear groups organised protest movements all over Western Europe.

# Student activities 3.

If you study exam questions and the syllabus covering the period of détente, neither the conflicts in Africa nor the Afghanistan War are described as "major themes" or "examples of material for detailed study". This can also be seen in previous exams. There are no questions asking specifically about the wars in Africa or about the Afghanistan War. So what you should prepare for is to discuss these conflicts as a part of ending détente and perhaps as a part of the reasons for the Second Cold War/end of the Cold War.

What is covered in the syllabus are "arms limitation" and "détente". Consequently it is possible to find questions discussing the reasons for détente in the Cold War. But there are few détente-questions. That is also the reason why this guide has only used 8 pages describing this period. This part cannot be omitted if you want to understand the "Second Cold War" and the end of the Cold War..

The 1970s can be compared to the 1950s. There was both détente and confrontation:

| Détente | Confrontation |
|---|---|
| 1968 the Non-Proliferation of Nuclear Weapons Treaty | the Tet offensive |
| 1969 SALT I talks start | The Prague Spring |
| 1970 The Moscow Treaty signed | US troops in Cambodia |
| 1972 Nixon visits China | |
| SALT I signed | |
| East and West German Basic Treaty | |
| 1973 US leaves Vietnam | 1973 Yom Kippor War |
| | 1973 coup in Chile |
| 1975 the Helsinki Agreement | North Vietnam captures Saigon |
| | Civil War in Angola |
| 1978 Camp David agreement signed | 1977 USSR deploys SS 20 |
| | Ethiopian-Somali War |
| 1979 SALT II signed | Islamic Revolution in Iran |
| | USSR in Afghanistan |
| | NATO announces the deployment of cruise and Pershing missiles |

The reason for including both the Indo China War and the Vietnam War in the "détente part" is that the Vietnam War ended in 1975 and its outcome is probably the single most important reason for the détente process.
You may get questions on a) how the Vietnam War affected the Cold War and b) how the Cold War affected Vietnam War.
What we can conclude from studying answer guides is:
- In many questions the examiner will help you by indicating what years you should cover.
- Study the question: If it asks how Vietnam was affected by the Cold War, use both wars. But if it specifically asks about the "Vietnam War", show that you know about the "Indo-China War" but use the "American" Vietnam War for your answer.

**Answer the following questions before answering the essay-questions:**

1. Describe Nixon's Vietnam policy.

2. Why was there a period of détente in the late 1970s?

3. What was decided in SALT I and II?

4. What was decided in the Helsinki agreement?

5. Account for Brandt's Ostpolitik.

6. In what way did the Middle East contribute to the decline of détente?

7. Explain Nixon's policy of linkage.

8. In what way did Africa contribute to the fall of détente?

___

9. What were the consequences of the war in Afghanistan?

___

1. How and why did Carter's foreign policy change in the late 1970s? (see also next part)

___

A number of essay questions will now be outlined:

13. Assess the role played by Vietnam in the Cold War.
14. How did the Vietnam War affect the Cold War?
15. How and why was there a period of détente in the 1970?
16. Why was détente brought to an end in the late 1970s?

Essay Title: **13. Assess the role played by Vietnam in the Cold War.**

Introductory points:

Conclusion:

**13. Assess the role played by Vietnam in the Cold War.** *(in this question you have to go through both "Vietnam Wars" chronologically. There is a lot to write here so don't overwrite but assess how this conflict affected the Cold War. The key word is "assess" i.e. show the importance. It doesn't necessarily mean that it was an important conflict)*

- The start of the conflict was mainly a **war of de-colonisation**. US support for a return of the French may be seen as a part of the Cold War, but notice that this US decision was made in May 1945. before the Cold War had really started.
- With the advent of communism in China, the new regime in started to support the Viet Minh in 1949. China was not prepared to accept a Western power and an ally of the US south of her border.
- The NSC-68 report in January 1950 advocated a substantial US military build up. The Korean War had not started but recommendations were affected by the development in Asia. China had been "lost" to communism and a full scale war had raged in Vietnam since 1946. With the start of the Korean War in June 1950, the US started to support the French in Vietnam. The **implementation of the recommendations of the NSC-68 report was affected by the development in Vietnam but it was far from the only reason.**
- China increased its support for the North in the 1950s. The Chinese feared the US would intervene. At the time of the Geneva agreement the **US paid for more than 70 %** of France's cost, showing the importance of the conflict.
- Stalin was more reluctant to support Ho in the war against the French. Khrushchev wrote that Stalin "treated Ho insultingly" when he visited the USSR in 1950.
- When **SEATO** was formed in 1954 one of the main aims was to prevent the spread of communism in South East Asia. **Vietnam was now seen by the Americans as a key country in the region**. The region provided the Japanese with important markets and strategically it was of major importance, hence the idea of the **Domino Theory**. If Vietnam was lost there would be a chain reaction throughout Asia.
- Both the USSR and China favoured a settlement over Vietnam at Geneva in 1954. China didn't want to risk US intervention on its southern borders.
- The importance of Vietnam was one reason behind the formation of SEATO. The formation of SEATO was seen as a threat by China. This was one reason why China started to shell some islands outside her coast in 1954 and 1955, known as the **Taiwan Straits Crisis**. The US threatened with nuclear weapons and signed a mutual defence pact with Taiwan. It is correct to conclude that Taiwan was more important than Vietnam in the mid 1950s.
- The formation of SEATO and Western presence in South East Asia in the mid 1950s was one important reason for the Bandung Conference in 1955 which would lead to the creation of the non aligned movement.. It was an attempt by Asian and African states to find a "third way" during the Cold War.
- **No priority was given to the Vietnam question from the communist camp in the late 1950s**. If Vietnam should be united it had to be through peaceful means. In the USSR Khrushchev had introduced his policy of peaceful co-existence and China feared a US intervention.
- When Kennedy came to power in early 1961 there were only 400 US military advisers in Vietnam. The evangelist Billy Graham met Kennedy in January 1961 and Kennedy told him that the US couldn't allow Vietnam to fall to communism. It was the first time Graham heard that Vietnam was such a problem. That ordinary Americans didn´t know about Vietnam doesn't necessarily mean that this conflict wasn't of major importance to the **Kennedy administration**. Both Kennedy and Mc Namara, the Secretary of Defence, believed in the **Domino Theory**. In the US it was believed that China stood behind the North and that the USSR stood behind China and controlled developments.
- In 1959 the North decided to unify the country by military means if necessary. In **1960** the guerrilla in the South, the **Viet Cong, intensified its activities**. Kennedy responded by increasing US economic aid and military advisers from 400 to 16 000 men in 1963.

- In the early 1960s, Khrushchev declared that the victory of socialism would be achieved through **wars of national liberation** in the Third World. Both the USSR and China now supported the North in its struggle and it was seen as a threat by the US. This was one reason for Kennedy's '**flexible response**' policy and Vietnam became a testing ground for flexible response.
- When Johnson started **to escalate the conflict in 1965** Vietnam became the **centre of Cold War** struggle in the world. In 1967 there were more than 500,000 US soldiers in Vietnam but no victory was delivered. It deeply affected the US economy and jeopardized her international role in the struggle against communism. It also undermined Johnson's "Great Society" programme and caused a lot of opposition in the US.
- As a response to the escalation, both **the USSR and China promised military aid** in 1964 and 1965. Due to the Sino-Soviet split there were no co-ordinated actions. These undertakings were of a massive nature. In the late 1960s China had 50,000 road and rail construction forces and anti-aircraft divisions in Vietnam. The Vietnam War led to a drastic increase of military installations in China.
- The failures in Vietnam led to a new US foreign policy. Nixon introduced his 'Vietnamisation' of the war and his Nixon Doctrine. The US needed to get out of Vietnam and Nixon realised that it was necessary to establish good relations with both the USSR and China. The new policy of **linkage and détente** had other reasons than only Vietnam, but this conflict was probably the single most important reason behind détente and it totally changed the Cold War. The US now abandoned her policy of a **communist 'roll-back'** and believed in a 'modus vivendi' i.e. a balance of power with the Soviets. The Sino-Soviet split showed that the communist world was no longer seen as one, monolithic, power where everything was led from Moscow. A "bi-polar" international situation was replaced by a multi polar view. The Cold War Triangle had been established and the Vietnam War and the US desire to get out of this war "with honour", had been an important part in this process.
- The victory of the North against the South in 1975 was seen by the New Right in the US as just another example of communist expansion and would lead to the Second Cold War which started in 1979.
- The experience in Vietnam made the Americans less willing to send troops to **Third World conflicts. In 1973 the US Congress had passed a bill, the** War Powers Act, restricting the President's ability to send troops to foreign countries without a formal declaration of war. According to the emerging 'New Right' in the US, this reluctance was cynically exploited by the Soviets in Africa and Afghanistan.

**Conclusion**: The conflict in Vietnam was of importance from 1946 to the early 1960s. But with the US escalation in the mid 1960s it became the most important Cold War conflict in the world. It had far reaching consequences to the US, economically, militarily, strategically and in her domestic policy. It was a driving force behind the détente process which would establish totally new relations between the US, the USSR and China, a Cold War Triangle. There are also those arguing that the legacy of Vietnam, a US reluctance to get involved in conflicts in the Third World, was exploited by the Soviets and would finally lead to the Second Cold War in 1979.

Essay Title: **14. How did the Vietnam War affect the Cold War?**

Introductory points:

Conclusion:

**14. How did the Vietnam War affect the Cold War?** *A similar question to question 13. But notice that it is asking for the Vietnam War. Show that you know the distinction between the Indo-China War and the "American" Vietnam War).*

- There is no definite starting point for this conflict. But start with Diem and how elections were cancelled. The formation of **SEATO** caused problems in the region and was probably one reason for the **Taiwan crises** in 1955 and 1956. Vietnam did not have a major impact on Cold War relations in the mid 1950s. Both the USSR and China wanted to achieve a peaceful unification of Vietnam in the late 1950s.
- There was an escalation in 1960 when the North decided to unify the country with arms if necessary. Both the USSR and China decided to support the North, anxious to maintain good relations with an important ally in times of Sino-Soviet disputes. This help in the **early 1960** must be described as **limited**.
- **The Kennedy administration never questioned the strategic importance of Vietnam**, hence they believed in the Domino Theory. But with limited fighting the US advisers were increased from 400 to 16,000 men. It is a significant increase but no combat troops were sent and the escalation cannot be compared to Johnson's.
- From 1965 **Johnson** started to escalate the US involvement by sending combat troops and starting air attacks on the North. As a response to this the USSR and China initiated with massive military aid. The Vietnam War was by now the **main trouble spot in the Cold War**.
- **The Vietnam War undermined the American position globally**. The Bretton Woods system - the leading role of the dollar in the world economy – collapsed. . The US soon suffered from inflation caused by the war and as a consequence faced her first balance of trade deficit in the 20$^{th}$ century in 1971. Worldwide the US was seen as an aggressor and lost support especially in the Third World. US credibility as a "champion of freedom" in the struggle against communism also suffered. If the US should be able to continue her leading role as a defender of Western liberalism, the war had to be brought to an end. The Vietnam War led the Americans to **reconsider her Cold War strategy,** to support détente. You could say that this was the first genuine US attempt to accomplish a détente process during the Cold War. But notice that the détente process was also due to Soviet nuclear parity and the Sino-Soviet split.
- With détente, **"roll-back" of communism was abandoned and the balance of power, an acceptance of communist sphere of influences, was established.** The US needed the support of both the USSR and China to get out of the war. China was finally accepted into the United Nations in 1971 and opened up after the Cultural Revolution. The US desire to end the conflict resulted in **better relations with both the USSR and China**. The Cold War in the 1970s saw new relationships and the Vietnam War was one reason for this.
- **US reluctance to get involved in a new conflict in the Third World** in the 1970s made the US more cautious. According to some historians and the New Right, this led to the Soviets to trying to extend their influence in Africa especially, but also Afghanistan.

**Conclusion:** It was from the mid 1960s that the Vietnam War had a major impact on the Cold War and in the 1970s it was one major reason for the détente process. It also led to US reluctance to get involved in new conflicts.

Essay Title: **15. How and why was there a period of détente in the 1970?**

Introductory points:

Conclusion:

**15. How and why was there a period of détente in the 1970?** *(Explain why it started and what happened)*

a) Why was there a détente process?

- **The Americans** needed to end the Vietnam War because it undermined their position both globally and domestically. US credibility to be able to fight communism, support in the Third World, the US economy and support for the president, all suffered from the war. The Americans realised that they needed support from both the USSR and China to accomplish their goal of ending the war.

- **The USSR** had finally closed the missile gap in the early 1970s. The cost had been astronomical. The stagnation of the Soviet economy started in the early 1970s and Soviet leaders realised that they had to slow down military expenditure. They were also attracted by the possibility of getting access to western technology, the US idea of linkage. The Soviets also feared the Chinese after border disputes in 1969. They realised that if they did not respond to American proposals, an understanding between the US and China could be a result.

- **China** was going through a volatile period during the Cultural Revolution. After the Warsaw Pact invasion of Czechoslovakia and the border disputes with the USSR they feared a Soviet attack. China was very isolated during the Cultural Revolution and the industry had suffered from this isolation and political purges. By turning to her enemy, China could gain both economically and strategically.

- In **West Germany** the Social Democrats and Willy Brandt wanted to establish better relations with the Soviet Union and her satellites. The idea was to overcome the **division of Germany and ease the tension in Central Europe**, rather than fight in the front line with the US in the Cold War. Better relations were needed with the USSR.

b) **Important achievements in détente (read more about each point in the text):**

**The Moscow Treaty from 1970** between West Germany and the USSR,

**1971 The Nuclear Accidents Agreement** between the US and USSR.

**1972 SALT 1** signed by Nixon and Brezhnev.

**1972 The East German-West German Basic Treaty.**

**1972 Biological Weapons Convention** signed by 126 countries.

**1973 Ceasefire in Vietnam and the American withdrawal.**

**1973 The Prevention of Nuclear War Agreement** signed by the US and USSR.

**1975 The Helsinki Agreement** signed by all European governments except Albania.

**1979 SALT II** signed. It went further than SALT I but was never ratified (approved) by the US Congress due to the war in Afghanistan. Both sides kept the agreement until 1986

Essay Title: **16. Why was détente brought to an end in the late 1970s?**

Introductory points:

Conclusion:

**16. Why was détente brought to an end in the late 1970s?** *(List the reasons)*

- **The Yom Kippor War** in 1972. The USSR had known about the attack but not warned the US. The Soviets were frustrated over the fact that Nixon's decision to place US troops on strategic alert had made it impossible to give crucial help to her Arab ally which then faced another humiliating defeat.
- The Soviets tried to extend their influence in the Third World in the 1970s. However Soviet influence in this part of the world was limited compared to US influence. Strategically the **USSR needed naval bases** in other parts of the world to be able to keep ships and submarines at sea. The Warsaw Pact outnumbered NATO as regards to the number of ships but could not take advantage of this as they didn't have access to naval bases, hence they were inferior to NATO which had bases in the Third World. Soviet expansion in **the Middle East and in Africa** can partly be seen against this background and was viewed with alarm in the US.
- In 1975 **North Vietnam conquered the South**.
- In Africa the Soviets gained allies. In **Angola and Ethiopia pro-Soviet regimes** were established after armed conflicts where massive Soviet aid and Cuban troops played decisive roles. There were pro-Soviet regimes in **Angola, Benin, Congo, Ethiopia, Guinea, Guinea-Bissau and Mozambique.** Other states had strong links to China. The USSR also established naval bases in countries in the Third World.
- In 1979 the USSR invaded **Afghanistan** and installed Babrak Kamal as president. The same year the pro-American **Shah in Iran** was deposed in a fundamentalist revolution, denouncing American influence. A radical anti-American fundamentalist revolution in the oil-rich Middle East threatened vital American interests.
- **In Europe right-wing dictatorships fell from power in Portugal and Greece in 1974, and in Spain in 1975**. In both France and Italy the communist parties attracted substantial support. All these states except for Spain were NATO members and it was viewed with alarm in the US.
- The "New Right" in the US concluded that the **Soviets cynically exploited US reluctance to intervene in the Third World after the Vietnam War**. A new US attitude could be seen during the Carter administration after the invasion of Afghanistan, and even more clearly when Reagan came to power in 1980. This view blames the USSR and her aggressive foreign policy in the Third World particularly for the Second Cold War.

There is an alternative explanation focusing upon the US and the "New Right" and **US domestic policy**. Fred Halliday represents this view. In his "The Making of the Second Cold War" he argues that the domestic development in the US was the driving force. In the 1970s the south and west in the US became more important economically and politically. Most of the military industries were concentrated in these areas and the electorate is normally more conservative here. The recession after the Vietnam War and the oil crisis in combination with the détente policy, had made the US militarily weak. Congress was dominated by the New Right and there were many conservative Congressmen with links to the military industrial complex. It has been estimated that 7 million people in the US were directly employed by the armament industry in the 1970s and politicians representing these groups had political reasons for discrediting the détente policy. It is partly an oversimplification to focus purely upon Soviet aggression. The US intervened in different ways in the 1970s. The coup in Chile in 1973 is one example. **It was the emergence of a new political right which was the driving force behind the process of ending détente, and not so much Soviet activity.**

# Part IV: The coming of the Second Cold War and the collapse of the USSR.

## Overview.

The invasion of Afghanistan was of major importance in ending the détente process. Carter came under domestic pressure and in 1981 Ronald **Reagan** was elected US president. Reagan decided to increase the strength of the US army and put the Soviets under a "systematic challenge". In 1983 he introduced the idea of a new defence system, the Strategic Defence Initiative (SDI). The Soviets were facing major problems. The war in Afghanistan and Reagan's systematic challenge all led to the **Second Cold War**. In the USSR the economy was stagnating and the old leadership had no solution to the problem. Between 1982-85, three Soviet leaders passed away: Brezhnev, Andropov and Chernenko. This brought a young and dynamic leader to power in the USSR in 1985: Michael **Gorbachev**. He soon introduced far reaching reforms both domestically and internationally. The reform process went however out of control and in 1991 the Soviet Union collapsed.

The **main aim** of this last part of the guide is to discuss the **reasons for this Soviet collapse** which brought an end to the Cold War

## The background – economic stagnation during Brezhnev but an increase of military spending.

The Brezhnev era is very important as a background to the problems in the early 1980s in the USSR. Brezhnev came to power after the fall of Khrushchev in 1964. After a period of collective leadership like Malenkov and Khrushchev, he soon emerged as the real leader of the Soviet Union. A long term consequence of the Cuban Missile Crisis was the Soviet decision to **achieve nuclear parity** with the US. This was achieved in the early 1970s but the cost was **astronomical**. The military competition with the US and her NATO allies put a lot of strain on the Soviet economy. **GNP in the Soviet Union in the 1970s was less than half of the US's GNP.** The border disputes with China caused alarm in the Soviet Union. In the 1970s the USSR kept 44 army divisions on the border to China while they had only 31 divisions in Europe. Consequently the Sino-Soviet dispute resulted in the majority of the Soviet army, totalling 3,7 million men, protecting a border next to a communist state. In the 1970s signs of stagnation in the economy were beginning. **The GNP growth had been around 10 % annually in the 1950s. It was 7 % in the 1960s and fell to 5% in the 1970s. In the early 1980s. the growth was around 3 %.**[79] The ageing Soviet leadership didn't realise that the Soviet command economy needed far reaching reforms. In spite of the détente process in the 1970s, defence spending actually increased. **Many signals** indicated that the Soviet Union needed a new policy with reforms, but they were **ignored by Brezhnev**. The fall of economic growth in combination with increased defence spending and military assistance to the Third World undermined the economy. Involvement in the Third World was dramatically increased: the USSR provided both Syria and Egypt with new arms after the Yom Kippor War in 1973. Cuban troops were transported to Africa in 1977 and military aid was given to both Angola and Ethiopia, naval bases were built in Africa, support was given to Vietnam in 1978-79 in a conflict with China, troops were sent to Afghanistan in 1979, in the early 1980 there were 25 000 military advisers in Cuba, Syria and Vietnam. It continued after Brezhnev with support to North Korea in 1984, and Nicaragua and Libya in 1985. **Brezhnev's ignorance of economical realities is probably one important reason for the collapse of the Soviet Union in the late 1980s.**

## Carter's policies.

**Carter** who came to power in the US in 1977, conducted a foreign policy with two faces. His early years showed **commitment to détente and far reaching proposals for arms reduction**. Détente should be linked to morality and the US should no longer support repressive regimes just because they were anti communists. In 1978 Carter cancelled the development of neutron bombs and he also signed START II in 1979. His later years are however normally described as the beginning of the Second Cold War, after the Soviet invasion of Afghanistan. This pattern of dualism was reflected in his two most important foreign policy advisers: **Cyrus Vance** was the new Secretary of State and believed in a continuation of détente and a new SALT agreement. He was opposed by **Zbigniew Brzezinsky,** the National Security Adviser. Brzezinsky, a native Pole, distrusted the Soviets and believed that it was only US strength that would make the Russians co-operate. Kissinger's old balance of power was rejected by Brzezinsky. The US should establish military superiority which was the only way to force the Soviets to change their policies. Brzezinsky stated: *"I don't consider nuclear superiority to be politically meaningless....strategic superiority can influence political behaviour. It can induce some countries to act in a fashion that sometimes can be described as a 'Finlandization'"*,[80] (i.e. to indirectly control a country through military superiority). He also believed that an expensive arms race would destabilise the Soviet economy. There were experts in the US who believed that the stagnating economy in the USSR in combination with policies in the Third World and military defence spending within the Soviet Union, were now bringing the country close to a collapse. Carter who was inexperienced in foreign policy followed Vance's line before Afghanistan but was converted to Brzezinsky's tougher stand after Afghanistan. Carter achieved some notable successes. In 1977 the **Camp David Accords** were signed between Egypt and Israel. Israel returned Sinai to Egypt and Egypt was the first Arab state to recognise, Israel. The Soviets had been excluded from the agreement. Relations were also improved with China and in 1979, Mao's successor Deng Xiaoping visited the US. Full diplomatic relations were established between the US and China in 1979. START II was also signed in 1979 but would soon be rejected by the Americans when the Second Cold War started.


## 1979 – a turning point.

1979 was a turning point and marked the beginning of the Second Cold War. The growing strength of the **New Right** in American politics in combination with the international development resulted in an enormous political pressure on President Carter. The hearings in the US Senate for ratification (approval) of the SALT II agreement resulted in a vigorous attack on the President's foreign policy. The SALT agreement was referred to by one Senator as *"appeasement in its purest form."*[81] In January 1979 the pro-American Shah of Iran fled his country and **Ayatollay Khomeni came to power** in an Islamic fundamentalist revolution, strongly opposing western influence and especially the US. In November the US embassy in Tehran was attacked and 53 Americans were held hostage for more than a year. The Iranian crisis led to oil prices tripling. In March a left wing revolutionary movement seized power in the Caribbean island of **Grenada**. In July the Sandinistas were finally able to seize power in **Nicaragua** and **in El Salvador** reformist military officers seized power. The USSR was not involved in the Nicaraguan revolution but Cuban advisers were there, playing a limited role. It was also announced that the US had discovered Soviet combat troops in Cuba. The troops had been there for years. When the Soviets invaded **Afghanistan** in December the same year, the US feared that the USSR was now extending its position in a very sensitive region: the oil rich Middle East. It was only years after Soviet and Cuban involvement in Africa and the USSR had now established close relationships with several African states. The development in Afghanistan made Carter finally support the Brzezinsky line leading to the Second Cold War. The Soviets disliked what they considered as Carter's zig-zag policies.

Notice that the view above about the Second Cold War was a US response to an increase in communist activities globally, has been challenged by Fred Halliday. He is arguing that the emergence of the New Right in the US was the driving force behind the Second Cold War. Most historians do however support the view that Soviets actions internationally, and especially in Afghanistan, led to the Second Cold War.

How did the US and Carter respond to this development? He declared in December 1979 when the Soviet invaded Afghanistan: *"My opinion of the Russians has changed more drastically in the last week than even the previous two and a half years before that."*[82] **The defence budget was dramatically increased**. Carter's two last budgets increased military spending from $174 billion to $200 billions. Reagan, who came to power in 1981 (he was elected in November 1980), increased it with an additional $ 32,6 billion in 1982 to $232,6 billion,. 13 % in one year. It brought an end to "détente with morale" and reintroduced the attitudes and the language of previous periods. In January 1980 Carter froze the ratification (approval) of SALT II and stopped US grain exports to the USSR. The Moscow Olympics in 1980 was boycotted. In January 1980 Carter announced *"any attempt by any outside force to gain control of the Persian Gulf region will be regarded as an assault on the vital interests of the United States of America, and such an assault will be repelled by any means necessary, including military force"*[83], better known as **the Carter Doctrine**. A Rapid Deployment Force was set up to deal with crises in the region.

**Ronald Reagan and his systematic challenge.**

**Ronald Reagan**

The Reagan administration was more than willing to continue Carter's tough stance. The Carter administration had been attacked by Reagan. In 1981 he said: *"So far détente has been a one way street which the Soviet Union had used to pursue its own aims…(and) reserve the right to commit any crime, to lie, to cheat…when you do business with them-even in détente-keep that in mind."*[84] Even though the US economy suffered from a recession, the 1982 military budget was increased by 13%. The USSR should be exposed to a **"systematic challenge."** New weapons should be developed which would be difficult to counter for the Soviets. New weapons would make Soviet weapons obsolete (out of date) which would put pressure on the Soviet economy. The Reagan administration started the largest peacetime military build-up in US history. Between 1981 and 1988 military spending went from $117 billion per year to $290 billion.

**Since 1977 the Soviets had been deploying SS-20** intermediate-range weapons in Eastern Europe. It was a typical Cold War strategy where one side tried to compensate for what was seen as offensive moves from the other side. the Soviets saw it as a response to US deployment of Thor and Jupiter missiles earlier (see the post-revisionist view and the "security dilemma"). In 1979 the US and NATO announced their **"dual track"** decision: new cruise and ballistic missiles would be deployed in Europe from 1983 if the Soviet Union did not dismantled their SS 20s. The new western missiles, **Pershing 2 and Cruise**, were a new generation of nuclear weapons which were both faster and more difficult to detect and very difficult to counter. They could be launched from mobile missile carriers. In the USSR it was seen as a major escalation. The Chief of the General Staff in the USSR, Nikolay Ogarkov, stated: the US is *"taking matters to a point of keeping the world on the brink of war."*[85]

In the early 1980s the Soviets faced a major challenge in Poland. Problems with the economy had resulted in the creation of an independent trade union **Solidarity**. In 1980 the Polish government recognised the union's right to exist in the Gdansk accords. The Soviet government was critical and stated that…*"the agreement…signifies the legalisation of the anti-socialist opposition."*[86] Preparations for an invasion were made but the Soviet leadership preferred the Poles sorted out their own problem. In 1981 the government declared martial law in Poland in an attempt to crush Solidarity. It led to a political crisis and the US responded with economic and trade sanctions on both Poland and the USSR.

The deployment of new nuclear weapons in Europe led to major demonstrations in Western Europe. In the USSR the leadership realised that this would put a lot of pressure on the European NATO members. In Geneva there were talks between the Americans and the Soviets, **the Intermediate Nuclear Forces talks (INF),** and the European governments in the west wanted an agreement where the Soviets would remove their SS 20s because then there would be no need for Pershing and Cruise missiles in Europe, which would satisfy the **peace movement**. There were also talks about a reduction of strategic weapons, the **Strategic Arms Reduction Talks (START)**. Germany was the key country. Brandt had been succeeded by Helmut Schmidt. He was faced by a difficult situation as an ally to the US: the grass roots of his party and many prominent leaders like Brandt and Bahr opposed the deployment of new missiles in Germany. Bahr stated: *"humanity is going insane…"*[87]

In 1983 Reagan announced his **Strategic Defence Initiative (SDI)** better known as the **"Star Wars"** project. The aim was to develop a totally new and expensive technology, a **shield** protecting the US in **space**. The SDI missiles were part of a defensive system which would destroy Soviet missiles before reaching the US by forming an **impenetrable shield. Few scientists took it seriously** in 1983 and it was seen as science fiction, but it was **difficult to totally ignore**. If the Americans poured money into an expensive research programme, it was possible that the SDI-development in the future would lead to a technological breakthrough, which would bring the Americans ahead of the Soviets. The SDI project played a major role in arms talks in the 1980s. It was a part of **"the systematic challenge"** of the USSR. The same year Reagan gave a speech which now must be described as "famous", to the National Association of Evangelical Christians. The Soviet Union was described as an **"evil empire"**: *"Let us be aware that, while [the Soviet leaders] preach the supremacy of the state, declare its omnipotence over individual man, and predict its eventual domination of all peoples on the earth, they are the focus of evil in the modern world. So, in your discussions of the nuclear freeze proposals, I urge you to beware the temptation of pride - the temptation of blithely declaring yourselves above it all and label both sides equally at fault, to ignore the facts of history and the aggressive impulses of an **evil empire**, to simply call the arms race a giant misunderstanding and thereby remove yourself from the struggle between right and wrong and good and evil."*[88]

Reagan's anti-communist rhetoric was very controversial in the early 1980s. But he was actually right when he described the depth of the inernal weaknesses in the Soviet Union. In a famous speech to the British parliament in 1982 he declared that the USSR was in the midst of a *great revolutionary crisis* and that *the dimensions of this failure are astounding."*[89] It would however take some more years until this became really clear.

**In November 1983 NATO started the deployment of the Pershings and the Cruise missiles. The USSR responded by pulling out from the Intermediate Nuclear Forces (INF) talks and START negotiations.** The Second Cold War had reached its lowest point. It was the worst year in the Cold War since the Cuban Missile Crisis in 1962.

It was argued that the difference between Cold War I and Cold War II was that in the West the Soviet empire in the 1980s, was not seen as an ideological threat any longer. The appeal of Soviet communism had been lost in the Prague Spring of 1968. The fear of the Soviets in the 1980s was purely militarily.

**Soviet problems.**

The situation in the early 1980s was even more complicated by internal problems in the USSR. In 1982 the ageing Brezhnev died and was succeeded by Yuriy **Andropov. Brezhnev** had not realised the need for reforms and to reduce the defence spending. The war in Afghanistan and support for the regimes in Cuba, Vietnam, Ethiopia and many others required enormous sums of money. The USSR suffered from a 'global over-stretching'. Andropov had serious health problems and was under medical treatment for most of his time in power. When Andropov passed away after only two years he was succeeded by another veteran, Konstantin Chernenko, a man known for being without qualities. Chernenko passed away after only one year in power in March 1985. When Gorbachev was elected General Secretary in 1985 there were many problems to solve:

- The economic growth of the Soviet economy had been going down since the late 1950s
- The Soviet Union spent 14-15% of its GNP on the armed forces. The US spent 4-6% (some new estimates are even proposing that it was 30 %)
- The gap between the GNP of USSR and the US was growing steadily and had been doing so since 1958.
- The Soviet society was lagging behind in the development of new technology, especially within computing. It was estimated that Soviet scientific computers were slower than their American counterparts by a factor of 20.
- Infant mortality was rising, the birth-rate was declining and average male life expectancy had gone down from 66 years in the 1960s, to only 60 in 1986.
- Revenues from the oil industry were going down.
- In Poland the situation was tense with the challenge from Solidarity.
- The war in Afghanistan didn't go well and discredited the USSR in the Third World and in the Middle East.
- Brezhnev's ambitions in the Third World had faced several setbacks, most notably Egypt and Iraq, but also in Africa. The annual cost for supporting Cuba, Vietnam, Ethiopia and Afghanistan alone was estimated to US$ 40 billion.
- China was still challenging the USSR as an alternative leader of the socialist camp.
- In Western Europe, Soviet communism was denounced by "euro-communists".
- Reagan was following a policy of "systematic challenge" of the "evil empire" and his Star War project worried leaders in the Kremlin.

# Gorbachev and the fall of communism.

Gorbachev

Shevardnadze

Michael Gorbachev was elected General Secretary at the age of 54 after Chernenko passed away in March 1985. He was the youngest member of the politburo and the first Soviet leader to be born in the Soviet Union and not in Tsarist Russia. He had been university educated and made his career in the post-Stalin era. It was a remarkable change of generation. Old hardliners and former Stalinists like Brezhnev, Andropov and Chernenko had now been replaced by an open-minded optimist and reformer. This drastic change of attitude can be best illuminated by how traditional Soviet political jokes developed. During the stagnation, the Brezhnev years, you could tell jokes about the leaders in private, but never in public:

*"Stalin, Khrushchev and Brezhnev were riding on a train when it broke down. Stalin's solution to this problem was to shoot the engineer. Khrushchev wanted to pardon the crew and give them a second chance – Brezhnev's solution was to pull down the window blinds and pretend they were moving".*

Jokes like these ridiculing the leaders were very common in the USSR. But as said above, you didn't tell them in public. With Gorbachev's openness things changed:

*"Two men were standing in a queue, trying to buy some food – an inevitable part of daily life in the USSR. One of them said: what's wrong in our country? Why do we always have to queue for daily food? His friend said: It's our leaders' fault. They are responsible. His friend said: I'll make them responsible. I shall go and shoot them!*
*After two hours he came back. What happened, his friend in the queue asked? Well, I gave up. The queue was longer there".*

What is remarkable with this joke is that it was told by Gorbachev – on television…

Gorbachev introduced a number of breathtaking reforms both domestically and internationally. He describes it as *"a complete renewal of all aspects of Soviet life, economic, social, political and moral."*[90]

Gorbachev's plan for reconstruction contained two main points:

1. Cooperation with the west to end the Cold War in order to reduce the costs for the arms race.
2. A reconstruction of the Soviet empire economically and politically.

It must be emphasised however that ideologically **he was a communist** but he wanted to reform communism in order to make it survive. Robert Service describes him as a Marxist-Leninist believer but he was very flexible and not in the least dogmatic. Gorbachev explained his new ideas in his **Perestroika, New Thinking for our Century and the World**: *"As Perestroika continues, we again and again study Lenin's work, especially his last...No revolutionary movement is possible without a revolutionary theory...this Marxist precept is more relevant today than ever."*[91] Some would argue that ironically his attempts to reform communism brought about not only the **collapse of Soviet communism** but also the **end of the Cold War**. In many ways, he reminds us of Alexander II, the "Tsar Liberator", who emancipated the serfs in 1861. Both Alexander and Gorbachev started to reform their empires but didn't realise that it was impossible to introduce liberal reforms in an autocracy or communist system. They had to learn what Tocqueville had written in *"L'ancien regime et la Révolution"* in 1856: the most dangerous moment for a bad government was usually when it began to reform.

Gorbachev realised that reforming the Soviet system required an agreement with the Americans on arms reduction. The Soviet Union couldn't continue to spend 15% of her GNP on her armed forces. McCauley writes that it was even worse: *"It (the USSR) had to devote about two thirds of its scientists and about one third of its economy to its military efforts."*[92]

| The USSR, and the world, now witnessed a number of daring reforms and initiatives: |

1985      Gorbachev made his first visit to the West, France, as Soviet leader. He proposed that the superpowers should reduce their strategic weapons by 50%.

1985      Gromyko, Foreign Minister since 1957, was replaced by Shevardnadze, indicating that a new era was to start. It had been impossible for Gorbachev to embark on his new foreign policy together with Gromyko.

1985      Gorbachev and Reagan met annually in four different summits. The first took place in **Geneva** in 1985. No major agreements were made except for the fact that they agreed to meet again. There had been no summits for five years so the meeting was important in establishing personal relations.

1986      The 27th Party Congress: Gorbachev announced that he believed that far-reaching economic reforms were needed and that the war in Afghanistan was a "bleeding wound".

1986      A nuclear reactor in **Chernobyl** exploded. The accident not only resulted in enormous costs for the government – it also revealed many of the weaknesses in the Soviet system. The government first denied the accident and denounced it as a creation of Western media. It convinced Gorbachev that far reaching reforms were needed.

1986      The second summit meeting between Gorbachev and Reagan in **Reykjavik,** Iceland, was an astonishing conference. Gorbachev announced that he was prepared to **withdraw** his **SS-20 missiles** from Europe, if the US withdrew their Pershing and cruise missiles i.e. an acceptance of Reagan's "zero-option" solution. It had until now been rejected by the USSR. He also proposed a **50 % reduction of all long range missiles**. In return Gorbachev wanted the Americans to call off the Star Wars project (**SDI**) but Reagan refused to abandon his project. Gorbachev then shocked the Americans by proposing **the abolition of all nuclear weapons** within ten years. Reagan's commitment to the SDI resulted in no agreement being made.

Geneva

| 1987 | The introduction of Gorbachev's **Perestroika**, or reconstruction and modernisation of the Soviet society. **Glasnost**, the policy of openness, was a second key word in the modernisation process. Past mistakes and criticism of leaders should be openly discussed and was encouraged. His book **Perestroika, New Thinking for our Century and the World** was translated into many languages and became a bestseller. Gorbachev met Thatcher twice in 1987 and the meetings were a personal triumph for the new Soviet leader. **"Gorbymania"** swept across the Western world. Thatcher said: *"I like him. We can do business with him."*[93] |
|---|---|
| 1987 | The **Law on Cooperatives** permitted private ownership of businesses in the service, manufacturing and foreign trade sector. Market economy had not been allowed in Soviet Russia since Lenin's days. |
| 1987 | The third summit meeting took place in Washington and the Washington Treaty (or **INF Treaty**) finally ended the dispute about intermediate missiles which had been a controversy for ten years. All missiles based on land in Europe and Asia, with a range of between 500 and 5500 kilometres should be destroyed within three years. It was the first nuclear treaty ever to reduce, and not only limit, the number of missiles. It led to **the elimination of one category of weapons** and also a detailed programme for **verification** of weapon destruction with inspectors. It must be emphasised that it only reduced the total nuclear arsenal by 5 %. Reagan was still not prepared to abandon his SDI project. It was Gorbachev who made the concessions. The "zero-option" had been accepted and it was Reagan who had insisted for a long time on verification of arms reduction. But Gorbachev was still popular in the USSR and he was now a cult-figure in the West. |

### 1988 THE REFORM PROCESS IS BEGINNING TO SPIN OUT OF CONTROL

| 1988 | Agreements between the superpowers were made in Geneva on the ending of the war in **Afghanistan**. |
|---|---|
| 1988 | The fourth summit took place in Moscow. No substantial agreement was made. The SDI was still a source of dispute. But the meeting had a symbolic value and showed that a new era had started. Reagan and Gorbachev were walking together through the Red Square, smiling. When Reagan was asked if the USSR was still an evil empire, he responded: *"No, I was talking about another time, another era."*[94] |
| 1988 | Later this year Gorbachev announced that Soviet armed forces should be **reduced by 500 000 soldiers**, without any demands on US reductions (a unilateral reduction). He also announced a gradual withdrawal of troops from the GDR (East Germany), Czechoslovakia and Hungary. No consultation had been made with defence ministry and Marshal Akhromeev, Chief of the General Staff, chose to resign the same day. |
| 1988 | Gorbachev announced that the USSR would no longer interfere in the internal affairs of the satellites. i.e. the **Brezhnev Doctrine was dead**. |
| 1989 | **Solidarity** was legalised in Poland. Later this year the Poles elected a non-communist Prime Minister – the first in over 40 years. This was a very significant step for the |

|      |   |
|---|---|
| | development in Eastern Europe. In Hungary it was declared that there should be multi-party elections. In September the **Hungarian border** with Austria was opened. The **Iron Curtain was falling apart**. |
| 1989 | The last Soviet troops **left Afghanistan**. |
| 1989 | In July Gorbachev addressed the Council of Europe in a famous speech: "...*any interference in domestic affairs...both of friends and allies is impermissible.*"[95] In this speech, Gorbachev again **rejected the Brezhnev Doctrine**, once declared after the Prague Spring. The satellites were free to choose their own path in the future. Some called it the "Sinatra Doctrine"; everyone "did it their way". |
| 1989 | Elections in the USSR to the Congress of People's Deputies. Voters were permitted to cross out names and 20 % of the communist Provincial Secretaries were not elected. |
| 1989 | Gorbachev visited East Berlin and declared that "*one cannot be late, otherwise one will be punished by life*"[96], which undermined the authority of Erich Honecker, the GDR leader. In October he was replaced by Egon Krenz. |
| 1989 | In November **the Berlin Wall came down** and in December Gorbachev met the new US president Bush, and declared that force would not be used in the satellites to prevent political development. Poland and Hungary were already moving out of communist control. At the end of **1989 communism fell in the other satellites**. |
| 1990 | Chancellor Kohl visited Moscow and principal agreements were made for a German unification. |
| 1990 | The first free elections in Hungary since 1945. |
| 1990 | The US and the USSR both agreed to end the Iraqi occupation of Kuwait, showing that the Cold War had ended and the superpowers were capable of co-operating even in the oil rich Middle East. |
| 1990 | In **October Germany was reunited.** |
| 1991 | The Warsaw pact was dissolved. |
| 1991 | In June, Yelstin was elected president of Russia, then one of the republics in the USSR, in free elections. |
| 1991 | In August an attempted coup against Gorbachev by communist hardliners failed. |
| 1991 | In December the leaders from Russia, Ukraine and Belarus declared that the **USSR no longer existed** and founded the **Commonwealth of Independent States** (CIS). Later the same month it was extended and eleven former republics joined the CIS. |
| 1991 | **START I** (Strategic Arms Reduction Treaty) was signed. This process had started in 1982 and was followed by START II in 1993. |
| 1991 | On 25 **December Gorbachev had to resign**. Without a Soviet Union, Gorbachev had no political platform. On 31 December the USSR formally ceased to exist. Yeltsin was the new leader in Russia. |

## Why did Soviet communism collapse?

The historical debate over the end of the Cold War is still in its infancy. It is a highly controversial and complicated question and historians are not likely to reach a final answer. The Cold War ended with the collapse of the Soviet Union. It is easy to understand the difficulties if we take into account that the answer to this question might involve issues like:

- Was it Reagan's "systematic challenge" of the Soviet system and his SDI which brought about the fall of communism?
- Is a market economy better than planned economy?
- Was it Gorbachev's far-reaching reforms which undermined the Soviet society? Did he try to reform "too much too soon"? A Chinese type of reform programme, where communism has been partly reformed (economically) could have resulted in maintenance of power.

There are mainly two different "schools of interpretation" discussing the fall of communism. One school explains it mainly as a **result of external pressure**. The other school explains the development as a result of **domestic problems** within the Soviet empire. Notice however that a combination between external and internal problems is possible. Let's study the arguments:

A. **External pressure:**

A 1. **Military reasons**

If we want to understand the fall of communism as a result of external pressure, we have to discuss the effects of the **arms race**. It's interesting to notice that the stagnation of the Soviet economy goes back to the 1960s. In 1958 the difference between the US and Soviet GNP was at its narrowest and after that the gap constantly grew wider. This was the time when the space race and the development of intercontinental ballistic missiles started. As a result of the Cuban missiles crisis, the Soviets decided to **close the missile gap** (see the Cuban missile crisis). The costs were astronomical:

ICBM = intercontinental ballistic missile
SLBM = submarine launched ballistic missile
ICB = intercontinental bombers

Source: Brown Money Cold War to détente p. 161

|   |   | **1964** | **1966** | **1968** | **1970** | **1972** |
|---|---|---|---|---|---|---|
| US | ICBM | 834 | 904 | 1054 | 1054 | 1054 |
|    | SLBM | 416 | 592 | 656 | 656 | 656 |
|    | ICB | 630 | 630 | 545 | 550 | 455 |
| USSR | ICBM | 200 | 300 | 800 | 1300 | **1527** |
|    | SLBM | 120 | 125 | 130 | 280 | 560 |
|    | ICB | 190 | 200 | 150 | 150 | 140 |

We can see from these figures that the Soviets were able to close the missile gap between 1964 and 1972 – but how did this affect other parts of the economy? It is of vital importance to assess what economic resources the Soviets had when they were competing with the Western world. What can we say about the size of the Soviet economy compared to the US (and her wealthy allies)?

GNP in $ US billion source Brown/Money Cold War to détente p. 164

| **Year** | **US** | **Japan** | **W Germ** | **France** | **UK** | **USSR** |
|---|---|---|---|---|---|---|
| **1952** | 350 | 16 | 32 | 29 | 44 | 113 |
| **1960** | 511 | 39 | 71 | 60 | 72 | 201 |
| **1966** | 748 | 102 | 123 | 108 | 107 | 288 |
| **1972** | 1152 | 317 | 229 | 224 | 128 | 439 |

Notice that the **GNP of the Soviet Union in 1972 was 38 % of the US GNP** - and only 21% of the US and her allies.

The economies in the Soviet satellites were far too small to play any role and due to the Sino-Soviet split in the 1970s, the USSR had to keep 44 army divisions on the Chinese border while they only had 31 divisions in Europe, so nothing was gained from having a communist government in China. The size of the Soviet economy was much smaller than the US economy while they were undertaking an enormous military build-up. **Consequently the Soviets had to use a considerable proportion of their resources for military needs**.

> Soviet statistics have always been a problem and have to be treated with caution. You will therefore find different estimates – but in general they say the same.

McCauley writes: "*It (the USSR) had to devote about two-thirds of its scientists and about one-third of its economy to its military efforts.*"[97] It is not likely that any state can afford this. LaFeber writes that the USSR used 25% of its GNP for military needs during the Brezhnev era.[98] Gaddis writes that the USSR had "*a defence burden that may have been three times that of the US by the end of the 1970s, when its GNP was only one-sixth the size of the American counterpart.*".[99] Crockatt writes: "*An additional burden was military spending, which grew from an estimated 10-12 per cent of GNP in the early 1960s to 13-14 per cent in the mid 1980s or even, according to some estimates, 18 per cent.*"[100] The most common estimate in the 1980s is 14-15 % of GNP was spent on military needs while 4-6 % was spent in the US. How did the Soviet economy develop from the late 1950s when this military build up took off? McCauley gives us some figures: **GNP growth had been around 10 % annually in the 1950s. It was 7 % in the 1960s and fell to 5% in the 1970s. In the early 1980s the growth was around 3 %.**[101] **It was negative during the later Gorbachev era** (-15 % in 1991).

Was stagnation due to the military development? Well, you will probably find different answers to this question but it is very likely to believe that **such an enormous undertaking had negative effects on the development of the Soviet economy.** Just to give another example, we have concluded that the Vietnam War had severe effects on the US economy in the early 1970s. It is possible to argue that there is a correlation between the costs for arms development and stagnation in the USSR.

How did the advent of Reagan affect the Soviet society? There was no drastic change in the Soviet economy with Reagan's coming. But the downward trend from the early 1960s continued. It is possible to argue that his "systematic challenge" and his SDI project convinced Gorbachev that far-reaching reforms were needed and that Gorbachev's reforms set forces in motion which led to a Soviet collapse. It is difficult to argue that Reagan's military build-up caused a sudden Soviet collapse. Signs of stagnation had been seen since the 1960s. George Kennan, the father of Truman's containment policy, found the idea of the collapse of the Soviet system as a result of Reagan's systematic challenge, as '**simply childish**'.

The war in **Afghanistan** was of major importance. Edward Shevardnadze, Gorbachev's foreign minister, said: "*The decision to leave Afghanistan was the first and most difficult step. Everything else flowed from that*". The Americans started to provide the Mujaheddin guerrillas with Stinger missiles in 1986. Stingers were very effective against Soviet helicopters and according to Crockatt "*it was decisive in making up Gorbachev's mind.*"[102] We have to add that the USSR kept 44 army divisions to protect their Chinese border while they "only" had 31 divisions in Europe. The **Sino-Soviet split** and the war in Afghanistan cannot be ignored when we are talking about "outside pressure" and how it must have affected military spending in the USSR. Military expenditure in the 1980s was far from just a struggle against capitalist states. Ball comments: "*A real Sino-Soviet alliance based on the convergence of political interests would have been truly formidable.*"[103]

## A 2 . Nationalism.

Glasnost or openness soon led to the abolition of censorship. It became evident that republics within the **Soviet Union and the satellites in Eastern Europe** were not satisfied with only decentralised power and democracy without independence. They wanted real independence. Freedom of speech released decades of bitterness over Stalin's repression and terror. In 1988 Gorbachev abandoned the Brezhnev doctrine and allowed the satellites to determine their own internal affairs. This is sometimes referred to as the "Sinatra doctrine" i.e. to do it "their own way". But he tried to prevent this development within the USSR. Anti-Russian feelings ran high and it became a test of Gorbachev's intentions and credibility. Nationalist feelings led to Soviet control of Eastern Europe coming to an end in the autumn of 1989. It also led to a number of republics within the Soviet Union becoming independent states.

## A 3. Influences from the outside world weakening the Soviet system.

The Soviet empire was influenced from the outside in different ways. The Russian population was attracted by Western habits and **consumer goods** which contrasted to the shortages and the queues in the Soviet Union. The Soviet system in the 1980s was eroded by Western influence and consumer goods just as the Tsarist system had once been eroded by liberal and socialist ideas. It has also been argued that the Cold War was already over from an ideological point of view after the Prague Spring. "Euro-communists" rejected a Soviet style of communism.

There were also spiritual influences like **Pope John Paul II** among Catholics in Eastern Europe and especially in Poland. When he visited Krakow in 1979, 2-3 million Poles were there to welcome him. . Gaddis writes that *"he began a process by which communism...would come to an end."*[104]

The influence of **Islam** became important in Soviet republics in Central Asia especially when the conflict in Afghanistan started. The Iranian revolution brought Khomeini to power in 1978-79 and even though there were different schools of thought in Islam, both the revolution in Iran and the war in Afghanistan were fertile grounds for radical Islamist groups, gaining more support in Central Asia.

### A 4. The collapse of oil prices

In December 1985 Saudi Arabia made drastic changes to its oil policy. In six months the production of oil in Saudi Arabia increased fourfold which led to a collapse of oil prices. The Soviet Union lost $20 billion per year. The reason for the new policy was that the Saudis feared that the Soviet invasion of Afganistan was a first step to gain control of the oil fields in the Middle East. The historian Richard Pipes, an advisor to President Reagan in the 1980s, has claimed that the US did what they could to keep oil prices low as a part of their policy of weakening the Soviet Union. The leaders in the USSR now faced a difficult problem because oil money was needed to pay for imports of grains to the USSR.

### A 5. Growing economies in the developing world undermined Lenin's ideas about imperialism.

Developments in the Third World further eroded support for the Soviet system. Countries that accepted Western investments and market economy had the fastest growing economies while countries with a socialist orientation were facing serious economic problems. Lenin's ideas about colonialism and imperialism were abandoned by economists even in the USSR.

> You must now be able to explain how "external pressure" affected the USSR.

### B. Was the collapse of the Soviet system due to internal reasons?

The Soviet Union encompassed one-sixth of the land area in the world and produced more oil, natural gas, iron, coal, lead, copper and zinc than any other country. Gorbachev writes in his memoirs: *"We had plenty of everything: land , oil, gas and other natural resources, and God has also endowed us with intellect and talent – yet we lived much worse than people in other industrialised countries and the gap was constantly widening."*[105] We have already concluded that that this was partly due to costs for military needs. But were there any other internal reasons?

### B 1. Planned economy did not generate growth.

Was the collapse due to the economic system of the USSR i.e. **planned economy**? Planned economy means that a large proportion of the economy is owned and controlled by the state. Thousands of state planners or bureaucrats decided what to produce, when it should be produced and at what price. It has been described as a rigid command economy. Industries were protected from both domestic and international competition. With a state controlled economy there were not enough private incentives. As an example this can clearly be seen within agriculture. Most farming was still collectivised i.e. state owned, but peasants were allowed to have small private plots. These plots made up 3 % of the arable land but produced 40 % of meat, diary goods and vegetables.[106] In 1990 the USSR had one of its greatest grain harvests ever, but 40 % of the harvest rotted or was eaten by insects .[107] The same problems existed within the industrial sector. Low morale and productivity harmed the Soviet economy. State bureaucrats and politicians decided where and how many resources that should be invested. It has been argued that these bureaucrats, the *nomenklatura* obstructed systematic reforms and new initiatives. It was in their interest to preserve the system and oppose decentralisation. Gorbachev wanted to vitalise and decentralise decision-making. This would of course undermine the power of the *nomenklatura,* so they obstructed Gorbachev's initiatives. Crockatt writes: *"a rigidity inherent in its ideology and institutions rendered it incapable of adaptability to change"*. They also obstructed new thinking in other areas. The USSR didn't understand the importance and the opportunities with **computer technology**. The Soviet system didn't foster any Bill Gates. It continued along the route of "heavy industry" as it had done for decades. It would never be the *nomenklatura* who would be a driving force behind a new technology. Gaddis writes: *"the computer revolution...thrives on individual initiative and an unconstrained flow of information, neither of which the hierarchical Soviet system was equipped to encourage."*[108] In the mid 1980s there were 30 million personal computers in the US and only 50, 000 in the USSR.

So does a planned economy generate a **lower growth** compared to a market economy? Mc Cauley concludes that large states are normally poor. There are two major exceptions and that is the US and Japan. Both countries have a market economy and are dedicated to expanding their export. Communist states had problems in generating growth over longer periods and neglected exports (or perhaps their protected industries couldn't compete on the world market?). McCauley concludes that *"only a market economy generates rising prosperity over decades."*[109]

So stagnation in the Soviet economy was due to a lack of economic competition, private incentives, entrepreneurship and the role of the *nomenklatura,* in obstructing reform initiatives. The economic system in the USSR was a very important factor behind the collapse.

> Explain how the system in the USSR weakened the country.

### B 2. Gorbachev made mistakes.

Was it **mistakes made by Gorbachev** which caused the fall of communism? Many hardliners in the Soviet Union argued, and still argue, that this was the case. While people in the West are still affected by "Gorbymania", he is blamed by many for what happened to the empire. Most historians agree that the reforms opened a floodgate which led to a collapse. Did he reform this iron-system too much too quickly?

What did Gorbachev actually do? Initially he emphasised the importance of discipline and blamed vodka consumption and absenteeism for the stagnation. But in 1986 he introduced his *Perestroika* or reconstructing policy, indicating that far reaching reforms were needed. Political parties and organisations were allowed. Censorship was abolished in 1988. Gorbachev's new openness was necessary for *Perestroika*. But it soon led to problems. Crockatt writes... *"Once given rein, the direction of the newly released force of public opinion could not necessarily be controlled."*[110]

- **The economy was transformed:**

The **Law on Cooperatives** in 1987 permitted private ownership of businesses in the service, manufacturing and foreign trade sectors. Workers were allowed to leave collective farms. Between 1985-1988 13, 000 producing cooperatives were formed and 300, 000 family- owned businesses. 50 % of the service sector and 40 % of agriculture were suddenly in private hands.[111]

The **Enterprise Law** transferred decision making from the central ministries to the enterprises. Managers in state owned companies were now given much more power.

The **Law on Joint Ventures** allowed foreign ownership of companies and Crockatt describes the effects as 'explosive'.

This dramatic reconstruction was a typical Russian transformation ordered from the top. The problem was that there was no well-established market mechanism and it led to chaos in both the old central planning system and the new capitalist system. (See figures about the economic development below).

Goldman argues *"shock therapy might have worked in a country where there were producers ready and waiting for the optimum market conditions."*[112] But this was not the case in the USSR. Companies had always been centrally controlled regarding what to produce. When Gorbachev now reformed from above; there was no effective system for capital investment, credit, fiscal and monetary controls i.e. institutions and administration necessary to organise a market economy.[113]

- **Political changes:**

In 1988 Gorbachev announced in the UN that every nation had the right to choose its own government i.e. a **rejection of the Brezhnev doctrine**. It didn't take long until both republics within the USSR, like the Baltic States, and the satellites in Eastern Europe demanded real independence. Gorbachev actually did his best to speed up the process in Eastern Europe, where many politicians opposed his radical transformation. In East Germany in 1989 he declared *"One cannot be late, otherwise one will be punished by life"*,[114] which undermined the authority of Erich Honecker. He was more reluctant to allow secession from the USSR by Soviet republics. But it was impossible to stop. **Glasnost, openness**, resulted in a revival of nationalism. Crockatt writes: *"Nationalism within the Soviet republics could hardly have been given voice had it not been for glasnost."*[115] There were 15 republics and more than 120 ethnic groups within the USSR and Gorbachev assumed that they would remain loyal if they were offered democracy. In 1990 **the leading role of the communist party** was dropped from the constitution and in March there were elections stipulating that officials must receive 50% of the electorate to remain in office. Many were swept away. In late 1989 communism collapsed in Eastern Europe and the impression was that it had Gorbachev's tacit support.

The détente process which was initiated by Gorbachev also deprived the Soviet Union of her **outside enemy**. It was this outside enemy which had justified economic hardship in the Soviet Union. Some would even argue that the outside enemy had been the whole *raison d'être* of the Soviet system. When the outside enemy then disappeared, the economy got even worse. It was very difficult to understand for Soviet citizens. Bell writes: *"Gorbachev was offending all kinds of vested interests, in the Communist Party, the bureaucracy, the armed forces and the KGB."*[116]

- **Lack of timing:**

There was no democratic tradition in the Soviet Union and no tradition of market economy. There had been a command economy for generations and the state had many times enforced its will by police action. Suddenly everything was more or less set free. The transition to a market economy was more difficult than expected. The liberalisation coincided with an economic crisis where incomes from alcohol went down due to Gorbachev's policies and, even more important, there was a fall in the world **oil prices**. So the political reform programme was introduced in a severe economic crisis. If Lenin once had "timed" the October revolution, Gorbachev did not time the right moment for this drastic transformation. We can understand the problems if we study the economic development:

**Soviet economic growth 1986-91 (%)**

| 1986 | 87 | 88 | 89 | 90 | 91 |
|---|---|---|---|---|---|
| 2.3 | 1.6 | 4.4 | 2.4 | -4.0 | -15.0 |

Source: Stagnation and Reform the USSR by John Laver p. 118

**In conclusion:** Gorbachev brought a) the conflict with the external enemy to and end and b) transformed the Soviet system.

> He only succeeded with the first point and must partly bear responsibility for the failure of the second point (economically). It was a utopian dream to offer freedom to the republics, when they were not prepared to accept the Soviet system. How should Glasnost co-exist with decades of bitterness over Soviet rule? And how should a decentralised economy co-exist with

the interests of the *nomenklatura,* the central planners? He tried to enjoy the best of two worlds in believing in market economy and the survival of communism.

How does Gorbachev explain the failure? *"I understood that initiating reforms on such a large scale in a country like ours was a most difficult and risky undertaking. But even now (it is) historically justified."*[117] He continues: *"The promise I had made to the people when I started the process of perestroika was kept: I gave them freedom...the removal of the monopoly on property and power...the end of the nightmare threat of nuclear war...(but) perestroika did not give the people prosperity, something they expected of me...But I did not promise that...I am at peace with my conscience. I like everyone else, made mistakes, miscalculated."*[118] He also writes: *"I thought we had a system that could be improved. Instead I learned that we had a system that needed to be replaced."*[119] Did he give up his political beliefs? It is difficult to know but he just had to continue the reforms: *"I'm doomed to go forward, and only forward. And if I retreat, I myself will perish and the cause will perish too."*[120]

> How did Gorbachev's reforms contribute to the collapse of the Soviet system?

It is possible to argue that the collapse of the Soviet system i.e. the end of the Cold War, was due to both external and internal factors. Let us list the main factors:

External factors:

1. The arms race/costs for military expenditure and support. The USSR had to devote too many resources to the military sector. The process of trying to close the missile gap started in the early 1960s and was a driving force behind the stagnation. Reagan's policies, especially the SDI project, probably accelerated this process and convinced Gorbachev that radical reforms were needed. But it was not the main cause of the collapse.
2. Cold War engagements in countries especially in the Third World were very costly.
3. The war in Afghanistan.
4. Nationalism in the satellites in Eastern Europe.
5. There were also spiritual influences from the Pope and Islam and, the attraction of western consumption, which should not be underestimated.
6. There was a drastic fall in oil prices in the 1980s which deprived the Soviet Union of resources that were necessary at a critical time.

Internal factors:

1. Planned economy does not generate a sufficient growth over longer periods.
2. Brezhnev, in particular, ignored the needs for reforms in the 1980s.
3. Gorbachev opened the floodgates of change which accelerated the demise. When his reforms were accompanied by a severe economic crisis, the system collapsed.
4. Nationalism in Soviet republics.

**Historiography:**

Many historians emphasise that the collapse of the Soviet system was due to an **internal collapse**. Bell writes *"The essential point still seems to be that they contributed to a drama which started within the Soviet Union."*[121] Dobrynin, the Soviet Ambassador in Washington, concludes: *"The fate of the Soviet*

*Union was decided inside our country"*. Shevardnaze, the Foreign Minister, agrees and points out that Soviet Russia once had survived WW II. *"Neither Hitler or Reagan could do it,"*[122] he said, talking about breaking up the Soviet Union from the outside.

The **key** issue is to determine to what extent this internal collapse was affected by **external factors**. You will find a wide range of explanations. Kennan, the father of Truman's containment policy in 1947, writes: *"The suggestion that any Administration had the power to influence decisively the course of a tremendous domestic political upheaval in another great country on the other side of the globe is simply childish"* and that the *"Republican Party leadership won the Cold War is intrinsically silly."*[123] The historian Richard Pipes, also an adviser to Reagan, found the statement astonishing and quoted Kennan in his famous Mr X article of 1947: *"it is entirely possible for the US to influence by its actions the international development, both within Russia, and throughout the international Communist movement"*. The idea behind Kennan's containment policy had once been based on the assumption that containment would *"encourage an internal implosion in the Soviet Union."*[124] Those supporting the view of the importance of external pressure, emphasise the importance of Reagan's 'systematic challenge'. But there are few historians who explicitly claim that it was Reagan who made the Soviet system collapse. Gaddis writes 'hanging tough paid off'. Did it pay off in a sense that:

- external pressure made the Soviet Union collapse?
- did it force Gorbachev to introduce his reform policy which made the USSR collapse?

Crockatt writes: *"The Soviet economy was not on the point of collapse when Gorbachev came to power. The catastrophic decline in the late 1980s was a direct result of Gorbachev's policies."*[125] But he makes a further distinction between "failures of the system" and Gorbachev's policies. Hence he is making a distinction between the two main points if we want to discuss "internal reasons": *"…the collapse would not have taken place* (a collapse as a result of Gorbachev's policies) *had not serious structural weaknesses existed."*[126] Gorbachev wanted to save socialism but would not use force to do so. Gaddis concludes that he could not achieve one without abandoning the other and that his goals were incompatible, hence Gorbachev made important mistakes.

It is however possible to find a **combination** between these two interpretations. External pressure affected the USSR but there were also problems within the empire which led to the collapse. McCauley concludes that *"monocausal answers are no longer acceptable."*[127] Bell believes that internal factors were more important than external factors, but he accepts that both are of importance: *"…the Soviet Union collapsed primarily through internal failures, exacerbated but not created by external pressures."*[128]

**To sum up:**

- One group of historians strongly advocate that internal reasons caused the collapse. **Evidence**: Write about the Soviet system and planned economy and Gorbachev's policies. Kennan supports this view.
- Another group want to emphasise the importance of external pressure. **Evidence**: Write about how many resources were used for military needs and that the stagnation started when the Soviets started to close the missile gap. The conflict in China, the war in Afghanistan, and influence from the outside world like western consumption and militant Islamism, and collapsing oil prices affected the Soviet system. Pipes supports this view.
- A third group support the view of a combination of internal weaknesses and external pressure and influence. McCauley, and many others, support this view.

> Different views are common when we are dealing with historiography. Historians are affected by their societies and, important for the Cold War, new evidence is made available affecting our explanations. "The origins of the Cold War" is one good example and "The end of the Cold War" is, and will be, another good example. What you have to do is to show an awareness of these explanations and how they can be supported.

While some would argue that Gorbachev partly caused the fall of the Soviet empire, we must keep in mind the positive achievements accomplished by Gorbachev. Without his daring initiatives it is hard to see how the fall of the communist regime in the USSR, the end of the war in Afghanistan, the development towards independence in Eastern Europe and arms reduction agreements, had been possible to accomplish in such a peaceful way. 1989 must be described as a revolution but almost no blood was shed. His attempts to reform the system in the USSR failed but without Gorbachev the end of the Cold War could have turned in a totally different direction. Russia is today a totally different country. Gaddis writes: *"Whatever ultimately happens to him, historians a hundred years from now will have much to say of – and probably considerable respect for – Gorbachev. They are likely to accord Brezhnev little more than a footnote."*[129]

# Student activities 4.

The reason for the end of the Cold War was that the Soviet system collapsed. Questions about the end of the Cold War are very frequent in IB exams. As we said earlier there are both internal and external reasons explaining the collapse. Most historians agree that internal reasons led to the collapse. **The key issue is to determine the part played by external reasons. We should conclude that external pressure was not without importance for the internal collapse. The reason for this is a stagnation of the Soviet economy from the time they decided to close the missile gap. We can also see that a significant proportion of the Soviet economy was used for military reasons. It is that it had a negative impact on the Soviet economy. This does not however mean that internal reasons were without importance. Hence we support the view that collapse was due to both internal and external reasons.** Historians have different opinions about the importance of each factor. It is a highly complicated question and it is only in the nature of the subject that there are different opinions. Try to find your own answer to this question and how you can substantiate your view – it is an important part of the process of being able to discuss the end of the Cold War.

It is likely that you will get questions where you will be asked to assess the importance of one factor in ending the Cold War, like: *"How important was détente in ending the Cold War?" (Détente in this context refers to a major degree to Gorbachev's initiatives).* This means that you have to discuss the importance of other factors as well. So there are a number of reasons explaining the Soviet collapse that you should be prepared to write a few things about:

**External factors:**

- Military expenditure caused the Soviet system to collapse.
- The Soviet Union was involved in many other countries in Eastern Europe and in the Third World, which put additional strain on the economy (this can be combined with the first point)
- The war in Afghanistan resulted in both economic and mental pressure.
- The Sino Sovict split.
- Nationalism in Eastern Europe and in some Soviet republics (mainly in the Baltic republics).
- Influences from the West concerning Western values. This includes religious influences from Catholicism in Eastern Europe. Influence from Islam was also important in Central Asia.
- Oil prices collapsed in the mid 1980s.

**Internal factors:**

- The rigid system of planned economy didn't generate sufficient growth and a revival of the economy.
- Gorbachev made mistakes when he introduced his Perestroika which led to the system collapsing.
- Brezhnev, especially, ignored the need for reforms in the 1980s.
- Nationalism in Soviet republics.
- Repressive policies by the regime had alienated large proportions of the population.

**Answer the following questions before answering the essay questions:**

1. Why are the Brezhnev years important if we want to understand the fall of communism?

_____
_____
_____
_____

2. What happened in Poland in the 1980s?

3. Explain Reagan's systematic challenge.

4. Why were intermediate-range nuclear weapons so important in the late 1970s and early 80s?

5. Explain Perestroika and Glasnost.

6. How did Gorbachev change Soviet foreign policy?

7. In what way did external pressure affect the USSR?

8. How did internal weaknesses affect the USSR?

9. How do you argue if you want to blame Gorbachev for the fall of communism?

10. What happened in 1989?

11. Why did Gorbachev resign in late 1991?

Finally we shall outline four different essay questions describing the main reasons for the end of the Cold War. As always, try to make your own outline and assess the outline in the guide because there is no "final answer".

17. To what extent did military expenditure lead to the end of the Cold War?
18. To what extent was it external pressure which led to the collapse of the Soviet system?
19. Was Gorbachev responsible for the collapse of the Soviet system?
20. Assess the importance of détente in ending the Cold War

**Essay Title: 17. To what extent did military expenditure lead to the end of the Cold War**

Introductory points:

1st main part:

2nd main part:

Conclusion:

**17. To what extent did military expenditure lead to the end of the Cold War?** (*Discuss the importance of military expenditure and compare this with other reasons*)

**Yes, military expenditure caused the collapse of the Soviet system:**

1. Write about the size of GNP in the USSR and how much was used for military needs (15-30 % of GNP). It is also a good point to compare Soviet GNP with GNP of US/allies.
2. Write about how the Soviets used resources for closing the missile gap after the Cuban missile crisis. A large proportion of her scientists were used for military needs.
3. Show how the Soviet economy began to stagnate when they embarked on the policy of closing the missile gap.
4. Show how engagements in other countries especially in the Third World consumed resources. The war in Afghanistan and the conflict with China put additional strain on the economy.

**There were other reasons which led to the collapse:**

1. Planned economy did not generate sufficient growth. This command economy lay behind the stagnation in that state planners did not promote new techniques and methods. It is not a coincidence that the Soviet system did not realise the importance of computer technology and just continued to plan for "heavy industry".
2. Gorbachev introduced too much too soon. After decades of repressive policies he suddenly allowed freedom of speech, Glasnost. There had also been decades of state control of the economy and when private companies were eventually allowed they had to co-exist with state planners who opposed Gorbachev's policies. Different nationalities within the Soviet Union used Glasnost to express their unwillingness to be Soviet republics, which led to a disintegration. By trying to control alcohol consumption the state lost revenues., Together with a collapse in international oil prices this led to a collapse of the Soviet economy. This sudden collapse was not expected by most experts and the reason for it is that Gorbachev introduced too many reforms within too short a time period.
3. There was strong support for nationalism both in the satellites in Eastern Europe and in some Soviet Republics.
4. Brezhnev must bear responsibility for not reforming the economy during the stagnation years.
5. Reagan's systematic challenge didn't cause a sudden collapse of the Soviet system. But you can argue that Reagan's increase in military spending, the SDI, support for the guerrillas in Afghanistan etc., convinced Gorbachev that far-reaching reforms were needed and that an understanding with the West was necessary. Reagan's policy is one important explanation of Gorbachev's reforms which led to the disintegration of the Soviet system.
Remember, Tocqueville had once expressed the danger of reforming a bad government.
6. The Soviet system was eroded step by step by outside ideas about Western consumption, culture and religion. Finally there was a lack of support for the system, even within the USSR.

Historiography: most historians support the view that the reasons for the collapse are a combination between different factors. However, there is a tendency to emphasise causes from within the system. McCauley writes that monocausal answers are no longer acceptable.

**Conclusion:** As has been written earlier, there are a wide range of explanations and there will be many "schools of interpretation" trying to emphasise different points. We support McCauley's view that it is a combination between different causes. In your answer try to emphasise what you think are the most important reasons.

| Essay Question: **18. To what extent did external pressure lead to the collapse of the Soviet system?** |
|---|
| Introductory points: |
| 1st main part: |
| 2nd main part: |
| Conclusion: |

**18. To what extent did external pressure lead to the collapse of the Soviet system?** *(This is a key issue among historians)*

**Yes, external pressure made the Soviet Union collapse:**

1. Write about the Soviet attempts to close the missile gap from the early 1960s and link it to the stagnation of the Soviet economy.
2. Write about the size of the GNP in the Soviet Union compared to the GNP of the US and her allies.
3. Write that a large proportion of GNP was used for military reasons. It is a strong argument to claim that this must have affected the Soviet economy in a negative way.
4. Write about Reagan's systematic challenge and his SDI project which put additional strains on the Soviet economy.
5. The Sino Soviet split made the Soviet Union place large proportion of her army to guard the border with China.
6. The war in Afghanistan was a military, political and economic disaster.
7. The impact of Western consumption and spiritual influences from the new Polish Pope and Islam in Central Asia eroded the support for the Soviet regime.
8. Strong nationalist feelings in the satellites challenged Soviet authority. In Poland the Solidarity movement challenged Soviet authority.

**No, internal reasons led to the collapse:**

1. Write about the Soviet command economy which didn't generate growth comparable to the growth of the market economies. The *Nomenklatura* also obstructed a modernisation of the Soviet system.
2. Brezhnev ignored the need for reforms in the 1970s.
3. Repressive policies from the regime had alienated a large proportion of the population. This was especially important in the Baltic Republics where many people wanted independence.
4. Gorbachev reformed too much too soon. It was difficult, if not impossible to allow freedom of speech, market economy and free elections in a society without any democratic tradition. He opened a floodgate of reforms in a situation where there was strong external pressure and where oil prices had more or less collapsed. He was tested in many areas. Let's look at one to exemplify his problems: How do you combine Glasnost or openness, Baltic nationalism and Gorbachev's desire to strengthen the Soviet system? Gorbachev's détente also led to the USSR being deprived of her "outside enemy". This outside enemy had partly united the country and justified economic hardship. The enemy had now disappeared but the economy collapsed. Few understood this.
5. There was a lot of nationalism in Soviet republics.

**Conclusion:** we support a combination between internal and external factors.

| Essay Title: **19. Was Gorbachev responsible for the collapse of the Soviet system?** |
|---|
| Introductory points: |
| 1st main part: |
| 2nd main part: |
| Conclusion: |

## 19. Was Gorbachev responsible for the collapse of the Soviet system?

**Yes:**

In 1985 Gorbachev became General Secretary of the Communist Party i.e. the leader of the USSR. For seventy years the communist party had organised a rigid system where freedom of speech, the right to organise political parties etc. had not existed. It was also a planned economy i.e. private enterprises were not allowed. Within a couple of years he had announced:
- In 1986 foreign policy versus the capitalists was fundamentally changed. Genuine co-operation and coexistence with the capitalist states was desirable. The "outside enemy" had for years been a justification for economic hardship.
- In 1988 censorship and the Brezhnev Doctrine were abolished. In the same year private enterprises were allowed.
- In 1989 there were elections to the Congress of People's Deputies where voters were allowed to cross out names of candidates. 20 % of the delegates were not elected. It was a significant step towards free elections in the USSR. In Eastern Europe the communist regimes collapsed with tacit support from Gorbachev. Hungary and Poland were the first to allow free elections which gave power to non-communist parties.
- In 1990 the directing role of the Communist Party was brought to an end by a change in the constitution.
- Far reaching economic reforms were introduced in 1987 and 1988 which contributed to the collapse

Gorbachev allowed a free debate, private companies, ended the communist party's monopoly of power, the satellites to choose their own governments and made peace with the outside enemy – after 70 years of iron rule. It was probably almost beyond imagination to most Soviet citizens. The difficulties were expected: the *nomenklatura* didn't want to co-operate in the destruction of their power. Nationalism was strong in many republics and in the satellites. It can be argued that it was too much too soon and that Gorbachev must bear responsibility for the collapse.

Crockatt writes that the Soviet economy was not on the point of collapse when Gorbachev came to power and that the decline in the late 1980s was a direct result of Gorbachev's policies.

**No, it was not Gorbachev who caused the collapse:**

- The Soviet system was doomed even without Gorbachev. Evidence for this is the stagnation of the economy which can be traced back to the 1960s
- No genuine attempts to reform the economy were made during the Brezhnev years.
- The basic problem was that planned economy didn't generate sufficient growth over a longer period.
- This internal weakness was exacerbated by external pressure (military expenditure, nationalism, the war in Afghanistan and Reagan' systematic challenge).
- Repressive policies had alienated large proportions of the population. Support for the regime had also been eroded by the impact of Western consumption and spiritual influences from the Catholic Pope and Islam. This was a long process which we can't blame Gorbachev for.

**Conclusion:** The problems which Gorbachev faced were to some extent caused by long term events and that the system had been suffering from internal weaknesses for a long time. Gorbachev's attempts to reform this system resulted in additional problems and contributed to the collapse because he had unleashed forces he couldn't control.

| Essay Title: **20. Assess the importance of détente in ending the Cold War.** |
|---|
| Introductory points: |
| 1st main part: |
| 2nd main part: |
| Conclusion: |

**20. Assess the importance of détente in ending the Cold War.** (*this means that you have to write about the importance o détente and also discuss other reasons for ending the Cold war*)

First of all you have to discuss the term détente i.e. lessening of tension between the superpowers. Détente was introduced with Khrushchev and Eisenhower in the late 1950s. This does however not explain the end of the Cold War. Détente from the perspective of ending the Cold War does become more relevant if we discuss detente in the 1970 and détente with Gorbachev and Reagan.

**Yes détente contributed to the end of the Cold War**:

1. Discuss the détente process in the 1970s.: the SALT-agreements, the Helsinki Accords and Ostpolitik. Right wingers in the US thought that the real outcome of this process was that the Soviets were able to expand their influence and the failure of the détente process is one explanation to the advent of Reagan and the Second Cold War (Haliday has questioned this view in his writings, see the end of detente). A lasting result from this period of détente was probably that personal contacts were established which would have some significance in the 1980s.
2. Détente with Gorbachev and Reagan: there are many examples of major events and agreements which finally brought the Cold War to an end: the annual summit meetings, the new foreign policy of the Soviet Union versus capitalist states from 1986, withdrawal from Afghanistan, the INF Treaty from 1987, the rejection of the Brezhnev doctrine, Soviet troops withdrawn from Eastern Europe and the unification of the German states. These agreements were accomplished by two politicians whom must be recognised for their achievements: Reagan was committed to fight communism but was flexible enough to make agreements with this "evil empire". It was Gorbachev who was the driving force in this process and his initiatives had a major importance in ending the Cold War peacefully.

**No it was not détente which ended the Cold War:**

Détente was necessary for the Soviet Union and Gorbachev if the reform process should succeed. What was it that forced Gorbachev to enter a policy of détente?

1. The cost for the Cold War was unbearable to the Soviet Union. The correlation between military expenditures and the stagnation can be seen from the 1960s.
2. Another problem was that planned economy didn't generate sufficient growth and that the Soviet GNP could not compete with the US's GNP. Détente was needed. These internal factors resulted in that an understanding with the west became necessary.
3. Reagan's 'systematic challenge' made an agreement with the West even more important.
4. The Chernobyl accident, the war in Afghanistan and a collapse of oil prices, made an arms agreement with the west even more important. Détente was needed.

**Conclusion:** Internal problems in the USSR made it necessary for Gorbachev to reduce military costs, if he should succeed with his *perestroika*. Problems in the USSR and external pressure made détente necessary, and détente led to the end of the Cold War.

# Part V: Germany and China during the Cold War.

Finally we will summarise how the Cold War affected two countries, Germany and China. The examples are chosen from two different IB regions. It is very useful in exams to be able to discuss one or two countries from a Cold War perspective. Most of the points that will be outlined below have already been discussed in the guide.

| Essay Title: **21. What role did Germany play in the Cold War?** |
|---|
| Introductory points: |
| |
| Conclusion: |

## 21. What role did Germany play in the Cold War? *(The aim is to show how the Cold War affected Germany and also how Germany affected the Cold War)*

1. With the defeat of Germany the most powerful state in continental Europe didn't exist politically and militarily. There was a power vacuum in the centre of Europe. Strategically this **power vacuum** was of enormous importance for the Cold War.
2. A number of war time conferences, ending with Yalta and Potsdam, formed an agreement where Germany should be divided into **zones of occupation**. An **Allied Control Council** where each occupational country had veto power should govern the country. A western zone in the eastern zone, i.e. Berlin, was a part of the solution. The **Berlin problem** became one of the most difficult problems in the Cold War because it opened up the Iron Curtain. Approximately 200,000 people fled each year between 1945-1961, until the Berlin Wall was erected. No final agreement was made over reparations and the Soviets were left to take what they could in their zone.
3. Co-operation between the occupational forces never worked. As early as 1946 there were signs of a political and economic division of Germany. Soon there were plans to form an independent German state in the West. **Byrnes's Stuttgart speech** in 1946 is one example of this. When a currency reform in the western zones was announced in 1948, Stalin decided to cut off all land routes to Berlin. The **Berlin airlift** was the first real crisis in Europe after the war.
4. In 1949 NATO was formed, partly as a result of the **Berlin crisis**. The same year a **West German and an East German state** were proclaimed.
5. From 1950 the Americans saw the rearmament of Germany as a keystone in their European Cold War policy. The question of allowing Germany to be a full member of NATO,. the creation of a German army, remained a major issue between the superpowers. Stalin feared this development and in 1952 proposed that Germany should be a united, neutral country. This was rejected by the West.
6. In 1953, when Stalin had passed away, there was an **uprising** against the communist regime in East Germany. It was crushed by the Russians with troops and tanks.
7. In 1954 formal restrictions for not allowing a German army were removed and West **Germany became a member of NATO in 1955**. The same year the **Warsaw Pact** was formed and **East Germany** became a member of this pact. From 1955 the two German states were rearmed.
8. In 1955 the Foreign Minister in West Germany, Walter Hallstein, laid down his **Hallstein Doctrine**: West Germany refused to recognise East Germany and would break off diplomatic relations with any government acknowledging East Germany.
9. In 1958 Khrushchev declared his first **Berlin ultimatum**: he demanded that all foreign occupation troops must leave Berlin within six months. If not, the USSR would unilaterally hand over the control of Berlin to East Germany. This would force the Western powers to deal with a regime they had not, and could not, recognise (see the **Hallstein Doctrine**). The deadline passed without anything happening. Khrushchev had been invited to the US and didn't want to press his point.

**10.** The migration from East Germany threatened the existence of the East German state. In August 1961 the **Berlin Wall was erected**. In October the situation was very tense and tanks from both sides faced each other for 16-hours at Checkpoint Charlie. The erection of the wall led to Berlin becoming less problematic from a super power perspective, the gap was closed.

**11.** In 1966 the Social Democrat Willy Brandt was appointed Foreign Minister in West Germany. In 1967 diplomatic relations were established with Romania, a rejection of the Hallstein Doctrine. It was the beginning of the "German détente" process: **Ostpolitik**.

**12.** Brandt became Chancellor in 1969 and he embarked on a more independent role versus the US, his Ostpolitik. In 1970 the **Treaty of Moscow** was signed between West Germany and the USSR. The existing frontiers in Europe should be respected, i.e. an acceptance that Germany had been moved 300 km to the west. The border with Poland, the Oder-Neisse line, was fully recognised by West Germany and Poland in the **Treaty of Warsaw** in 1970. In the **Four-Power-Agreement** the occupational powers of Germany recognised their joint rights to Berlin. **The East German-West German Basic Treaty from 1972** was a formal recognition of two German states and the links from West Germany to West Berlin were accepted. The Helsinki agreement from 1975 also recognised the existing borders in Europe.

**13.** In 1977 the Soviets started to deploy their new **medium range missiles, SS 20s**, in central Europe. They could not reach the US but could target her allies in Europe, such as Germany. After long negotiations the US and her allies in Europe started to deploy Pershing missiles in Western Europe. It led to public protests in many countries including West Germany. Brandt openly sided with the anti-war movement and it led to a major split in German society.

The opposition to the deployment of Pershing II missiles in Europe led to a mass **peace movement** and a **split** of the Social Democratic Party in West Germany. The Western powers wanted the USSR to withdraw their SS20s, if the deployment of Pershings was cancelled. West Germany became a very important **mediator** between the US and the USSR. Chancellor Schmidt concluded: the Federal Republic gained world-wide importance never achieved before.

The German Chancellor Schmidt concluded that unrest and fear in the world and in Europe affected and endangered German-German cooperation: there were problems in Afghanistan, Africa and, next to Germany, Poland. If problems earlier in Germany had affected the Cold War, it was global problems in the late 1980s problems that affected the détente process in Germany.

The Social Democrats lost the elections in 1983 and the new Christian Democrat government led by Chancellor Kohl accepted the missiles. Kohl did his best to preserve good relations with the USSR and continue rapprochement. How important was this missile crisis in a Cold War perspective? The historian Ball concludes that the most serious threat to the Western alliance came with the Euromissile crisis of 1979-83.

**14.** In the autumn of 1989 the communist regime in **East Germany collapsed**. During the night of 9-10 November the Berlin Wall was knocked down. It had tacit support from Gorbachev.

**15.** In March 1990 there were free elections in East Germany. The communist party got 16 % support, while the Social Democrats got 22 % and the Christian Democrats 48 % of the votes. In July in a meeting with Chancellor Kohl, Gorbachev accepted a German unification. In the **Two plus Four agreement** the four occupational powers and the two German states accepted a **re-unification** which took place on the 3 October 1990. Was this the real end of the Cold War?

**Conclusion**: One can conclude that it was the Cold War which affected Germany. One exception was Brandt and his Ostpolitik which had an effect on the Cold War, i.e an example where Germany affected the Cold War.

**Essay Title: 22. What role did China play in the Cold War?**

Introductory points:

Conclusion

**22. What role did China play in the Cold War?**

1. Between 1945-49 the Civil War restarted between the Nationalists and the Communists. It didn't become a major Cold War event. The US initially provided the Nationalists with weapons but sent no combat troops. The importance of China was clear: it did become one of five permanent members of the Security Council in the UN – represented by the Nationalist government.
2. In 1949 The Peoples Republic of China was proclaimed. In 1950 the **Sino-Soviet Friendship Treaty** was signed, and China was now considered by the West as as a part of the "Russian bloc". But Mao was never Stalin's client. Mao described China as a part of a "vast intermediate zone", meaning that China did not belong to the USSR or the US. But China needed Soviet help and the early 1950s was referred to as "the leaning to one side" period in China. Mao realised that Soviet help was needed for the reconstruction of China and to conquer Taiwan.
3. Late in 1950 the Chinese decided to intervene in the **Korean War**. That the Chinese actively and successfully fought the Americans in Korea 1950-53 had major implications. The Americans now implemented their NSC-68 plan which led to a major **global** military build up. China gained prestige in the Third World but was now isolated diplomatically and closely tied to the USSR. The war also led to firm commitments from the US to **Taiwan** and the French in **Indochina**.
4. The Chinese stood behind the Viet Minh in **Vietnam** from the early 1950s. It is probable that without this Chinese support the Viet Minh had not been able to fight foreign intervention as successfully as they did.
5. China was seen by the Americans as a driving force behind both the Korean War and the Indo-China War. The development in the region led to the formation of SEATO in 1954.
6. There were two major crises in Sino-American relation in the mid 50s. There are some small **islands in the Taiwan Straits** between Taiwan and China, called Quemoy and Matsu islands. In 1954 the leader in Taiwan threatened China with a "holy war". China responded with an artillery bombardment in late 1954 and early 1955. The crisis led to a renewed US pledge to defend Taiwan. When the Chinese conquered another island, Tachen, the US Congress passed a resolution allowing Eisenhower to take whatever actions he found necessary. Eisenhower announced that aggression from the communists would be met by nuclear arms. In 1958 there were new bombardments and again the **US threatened with the use of nuclear arms.**
7. In 1959 the USSR decided to pull out of an agreement where they had promised to provide China with nuclear technology. This process had taken two years and Mao reacted strongly. The nuclear issue was one of he reasons for the Sino-Soviet split.
8. The Great Leap Forward and the Cultural Revolution represents a period in Chinese history were she was **isolated** and was **opposing both the US and the USSR**. In 1964 she exploded her first atomic bomb and probably the most likely target was the USSR.
9. The **rapprochement to the US** in 1971 had major **Cold War implications**, from a Chinese perspective only comparable with the Korean War. That China was turning to the US sent **shock waves through the USSR**. A deep understanding between China and the US would totally isolate the USSR. It made the Soviets fully embark on the **détente** policy with the US. China was now accepted in the UN and there was Chinese support for bringing an end to the Vietnam War.

**10.** In 1972 **Nixon visited China**. In a joint declaration the Chinese stated that there was only one legal Chinese government and that Taiwan was one of its provinces. The US acknowledged that there was only **one China** and that they ultimately would withdraw their forces from Taiwan.

**11.** In the late 1970s **Deng** had become the real leader of China. In 1978 the US broke off diplomatic relations with Taiwan and ended their defence agreement. China promised not to use force to unite the country. **The US gave full diplomatic recognition to China from 1 January 1979**. The Chinese thought that the US would control the USSR so it would not turn on China. This development angered the USSR and led to complications in the SALT II negotiations. Sino-American cooperation was seen as a danger in the USSR. In the 1970s the Soviets had more troops guarding the Chinese border than they had in Europe. The Sino-Soviet split had major implications in the 1970s and 1980s. China and the US supported the FNLA in Angola while the Soviets supported the MPLA. In 1978 Vietnam invaded Cambodia. The USSR supported Vietnam while Cambodia was supported by China. China even attacked Vietnam. The triangular relationship between the three great powers of the Cold War continued under Deng in the early 1980s.

**12.** China embarked on her policy of **modernisation** in the 1980s under the leadership of Deng and maintained **good relations with the US**. China and the US shared intelligence on the USSR and the US also started to export military equipment to China in 1980. The Reagan administration continued this policy. When the Soviet system started to deteriorate in the mid 1980s, the **USSR was no longer seen as a immediate threat**. Diplomatic relations were established at senior level and relations improved. In 1989 Gorbachev went to Beijing in an attempt to end the Sino-Soviet split. The visit took place amid mounting student demonstrations for democracy (which led to the massacre at Tienanmen square) but Gorbachev concluded that their relationship had reached a 'new stage'. China found her way out of the Cold War during the period of détente in the late 1980s while the USSR finally disintegrated.


**China affected the outside world during the Cold War. The Korean War and rapprochement with the US were most important. The "Cold War triangle" was of major importance to China's Cold War relations. The Sino Soviet split which started in the late 1950s is vital if you want to understand China during the Cold War.**

# Part VI: The nuclear arms race and the major arms agreement.

In 1945 the Americans exploded the first atomic bomb, and were followed by the Soviets in 1949. Soon, both superpowers developed hydrogen bombs. The next step was to develop ballistic missiles in the late 1950s. These missiles were soon installed on submarines. In the 1970s individual missiles were equipped with multiple warheads. The 1970s also saw the development of anti-missile systems. Cruise missiles were created to fly low and hit their targets. Arms development is important and the main events and arms agreements will now be summarised:

| Essay Title: **23. What were the main events in the arms race 1945-1991?** |
|---|
| Introductory points: |

## 23. What were the main events in the arms race 1945-1991?

**1945: The first atomic bombs** were used against the Japanese cities of Hiroshima and Nagasaki. It ended WW II and, according to some, started the Cold War.

**1949: The USSR** exploded their first bomb.

**1952**: The US exploded their first **hydrogen bomb** and the year after the Russians did the same. In **1952 Britain** exploded their first atomic bomb.

**1957**: The USSR shocked the Americans by launching an **ICBM and a satellite into the space**. The Americans followed months after.

**1960**: First **submarines** equipped with nuclear missiles. They could remain submerged for two months.
**1960:** France became a nuclear power.
**1964 The Test Ban Treaty,** signed by the US and USSR, prohibited nuclear tests in the atmosphere, in outer space and under water
After the Cuban Missile Crisis the Soviets decided to **close the missile gap** and to attain parity with the US, which they achieved in the early 1970s.
**1964: The Chinese** exploded their first bomb.

**1968: The Non-Proliferation of Nuclear Weapons Treaty** sign by the US, the USSR and Britain. Nuclear technology should not be transferred to other countries. France and China did not sign.

**1972 SALT I** signed. It comprised two treaties:
- **The Anti-Ballistic Missile Treaty (ABM).** The number of ABM systems was limited to two each as it was considered that an effective anti ballistic system could make one aggressor more tempted to start an attack (the ABM system would defend the aggressor)
- **The Interim Agreement on Offensive Arms.** There should be a five year freeze on levels of ICMBs and SLBMs. There were no limits on strategic long-range bombers or MIRVs (Multiple Independently targetable Re-entry Vehicles)

The SALT agreement was a recognition of Soviet nuclear equality. It was also a recognition that a nuclear war would mean the destruction of both, hence a war must by avoided at any cost. This was referred to as **Mutual Assured Destruction**. This was the idea behind the terror balance: fear of nuclear destruction would lead to peace.

**1979 SALT II.** This agreement went further than SALT I. It limited the number of ICBMs and SLBMs to 2,400 each and included a ceiling on the number of MIRVs. It was not ratified by the US Congress due to the invasion of Afghanistan but both governments kept to the agreement until 1986.

**There was a new arms race in the 1970s. In 1977 the USSR started to deploy SS-20** intermediate-range weapons in Eastern Europe. The Soviets saw this as a response to activities from the US and NATO. NATO responded by deploying Pershing 2 and Cruise missiles in Western Europe. It led to years of discussions and anti-war demonstrations in Western Europe. The Western Alliance started this deployment in 1983 despite the protests .

**1982 START, Strategic Arms Reduction Talks** started while the dispute on medium range missiles was going on. The USSR called it off in 1983 when the first US Pershings were deployed in Europe.

**1983 Reagan launches his SDI project. After 1985** Gorbachev was prepared to make far-reaching reductions of nuclear arms if Reagan gave up his SDI project – which he refused.

**1987** The Washington Treaty (or **INF Treaty**) finally ended the dispute about intermediate missiles which had been a controversy for ten years. All missiles based on land in Europe and Asia with a range of between 500 and 5,500 kilometres should be destroyed within three years. It was the first nuclear treaty ever to reduce, and not only limit, the number of missiles. It led to **the elimination of one category of weapons** and also a detailed programme for verification of weapon destruction by inspectors. We should empahsise that it only reduced the total nuclear arsenal by 5 %.

**1991 The signing of the START I Treaty** which reduced the number of Soviet long-range nuclear warheads from 11,012 to 6,163 and US warheads from 12,646 to 8,556. The Cold War was now fading away. In 1991, the same year, the Warsaw Pact was dissolved. Gorbachev resigned on 25 December and the Soviet Union ceased to exist on 31 December 1991.
**Notice:** START I was followed by START II in 1993 which reduced the number of warheads to 3,000-3,500 on each side, by one-third. These two treaties resulted in substantial reductions of long range nuclear weapons. When one adds the INF agreement from 1987 abolishing all medium range missiles, the two sides achieved a lot. SALT I and II didn't reduce the number of weapons. It only put a ceiling on the maximum number of weapons

Finally let's summarise the development of the number of long range nuclear weapons. The arms race didn't end with the Soviets reaching parity in the early 1970s. Nor is it possible to trace the economic collapse of the USSR in the 1980s in these figures (notice that no figures exist for START I from 1991):

Source Brown Mooney Cold War to détente.

|      |      | 1964 | 1968 | 1970 | 1972 | 1980 | 1990 |
|------|------|------|------|------|------|------|------|
| US   | ICBM | 834  | 1054 | 1054 | 1054 | 1039 | 990  |
|      | SLBM | 416  | 656  | 656  | 656  | 576  | 624  |
| USSR | ICBM | 200  | 800  | 1300 | 1527 | 1330 | 1710 |
|      | SLBM | 120  | 130  | 280  | 560  | 937  | 930  |

# Further reading:

One source that represents the **orthodox view** is Arthur M **Schlesinger** Jr's *"Origins of the Cold War"*, Foreign Affairs 46 (1967). A useful book covering the whole Cold War written by a leading **revisionist** is **Walter LaFeber's** *"America, Russia and the Cold War, 1945-2002"*. This book can also be used as a course book. **Post-revisionism** can be represented by **John Lewis Gaddis** and *"The United States and the Origins of the Cold War"*. His *"We Now Know" – rethinking the Cold War*, (1997), is an analysis of the Cold War from its origins to the Cuban Missile Crisis and it includes new archival evidence from the Soviet bloc. His view on Stalin must be described as historiographically "orthodox".

Martin **McCauley** has written books explaining both the origins and the end of the Cold War and includes many useful primary documents: *The Origins of the Cold War 1941-1949* and *Russia, America and the Cold War*.

Other possible course books covering the whole period are: *"The World since 1945, an International History"* by P M H **Bell** which is a very well written book about the Cold War. A simular book with the same title is *"The World since 1945"* by C **McWilliams** and H **Piotrowski**. "The Cold War" by S J **Ball** is a very good and useful source with many first hand accounts from key individuals from the Cold War. Richard **Crockatt's** book *"The Fifty Years War"* is a very well written account about the Cold War. There are many references to scholars who have investigated different Cold War issues. It is a very good source if you want to get information about where to find different in-depth studies for Historical Investigations or Extended Essays.**David Williamson** has written a text book for A-level use, *"Europe and the Cold War 1945-91"*

If you want to find documents from the Cold War, J **Hanimäki** and O A **Westad**'s *The Cold War- A History in Documents and Eyewitness Accounts"* is a very useful source. There are also many useful internet sources: The **Avalon project** at Yale Law Schools has published a number of documents in history and diplomacy and we strongly recommend is http://www.yale.edu/lawweb/avalon/avalon.htm. A very interesting source is the **"America Rhetoric"** site where you can both read and listen to many speeches made by American decision makers (http://americanrhetoric.com/). **The Cold War International History Bulletin (CWIHP) at Woodrow Wilson International Center for Scholars** provides you with hundreds of documents and in-depth articles from archives and scholars discussing Cold War history. You can find it at **www.cwihp.si.edu/**. It is a vey useful source for Historical Investigations and Extended Essays.

There are always conflicts that attract more attention than others. The Cuban missile crisis is one. An absolutely outstanding source analysing this conflict is **Lebow and Stein**, *"We all lost the Cold War"* and another very special source showing the unique conversations in the Excomm is: **The Kennedy Tapes: Inside the White House During the Cuban Missile Crisis** by *Ernest Zelikow and Philip M*ay.

There are accounts written by key decision makers during the Cold War which are very interesting, despite their obvious limitations concerning objectivity. **Khrushchev**'s memoirs *"Khrushchev remembers"*, is a very common source in Paper I and fascinating to read. Michael **Gorbachev**'s *"memoirs"* is another interesting source. A comparable source is Henry **Kissinger**'s *"American Foreign Policy"*. **Robert Kennedy's** *"Thirteen Days"* gives us his story about the Cuban crisis. There are almost unlimited sources written by key decision makers: Brezezinski, Bush, Carter, Churchill, Dobrynin, Ford, Kennan, Nixon, Reagan, Sadat, Shultz and Thatcher all wrote their political "story".

Finally the best and most useful television documentary is **CNN**'s *"The Cold War."*

[1] Why Lenin Why Stalin? Why Gorbachev? Longman, New York 1993, p. 117
[2] Gaddis J L, We now know, rethinking the Cold War, Oxford University press, Oxford 1997, p. 1
[3] Mc Cauley M, The Origins of the Cold War, Longman Group Limited, Harlow 1995, p.119
[4] ibid p. 118
[5] The Avalon project, Yale Law School: http://www.yale.edu/lawweb/avalon/avalon.htm
[6] ibid
[7] ibid
[8] ibid
[9] ibid
[10] ibid
[11] Mc Cauley, The Origin of the Cold War, p. 110
[12] Gaddis J L, We know now, rethinking the Cold War, p. 292
[13] Mc Cauley, The Origin of the Cold War, p. 112
[14] ibid p. 113
[15] Hanhimäki and Westad, The Cold War, A History in Documents, Oxford University press, Oxford 2003, p 111
[16] Crockatt R, The Fifty Years War, Routledge, London 1995, p. 74
[17] McCauley, The Origins of the Cold War, p 132-133
[18] ibid p. 133
[19] ibid p 135
[20] ibid p138
[21] Rayner, The Cold War, Hodder and Stoughton, London 1992, p.16
[22] Hanimäki and Westad, The Cold War, p. 126-128
[23] Edwards O, The USA and the Cold War, Hodder & Stoughton Educational, London 1992, p. 50
[24] Rayner, The Cold War, p. 21
[25] Ball S J, The Cold War, Arnold, London 1998, p. 17
[26] McCauley M, Russia, America and the Cold War, Pearson Education Lilited, Harlow 2003 p. 38
[27] ibid p.48
[28] Edwards O, The USA and the Cold War, p. 68
[29] ibid p. 80
[30] McCauley M, Russia, America and the Cold War p. 184
[31] Khrushchev N, Khrushchev remembers, Little Brown and Company, Boston 1972, p. 600
[32] Ball, The Cold War, p. 152
[33] The Economist, July 29th 2006, p.24
[34] Williamson D, Europe and the Cold War 1945-91 Second edition, Hodder Murray, London 2006, p. 123
[35] Khrushchev, Khrushchev remembers, p. 453
[36] Ibid p. 456
[37] Edwards O, The USA and the Cold War, p. 114
[38] Khrushchev, Khrushchev remembers, p 460
[39] ibid p 460
[40] Hanimäki and Westad, The Cold War, p. 331
[41] Ball, The Cold War, p. 72
[42] Lebow and Stein, We all lost the Cold War, Princeton University Press, New Jersey 1994, p.
[43] ibidp. 35
[44] http://americanrhetoric.com/speeches/jfkinaugural.htm
[45] Hanimäki and Westad, The Cold War, p. 359
[46] ibid p 291
[47] http://www.yale.edu/lawweb/avalon/monroe.htm
[48] ibid
[49] http://en.wikiquote.org/wiki/Theodore_Roosevelt
[50] http://www.yale.edu/lawweb/avalon/decade/decad061.htm
[51] Lebow and Stein, We all lost the Cold War, p. 25
[52] ibid p. 30
[53] Khrushchev remembers, p. 494
[54] ibid p.493
[55] Lebow and Stein, We all lost the Cold War, p. 43
[56] Khrushchev, Khrushchev remembers, p.500
[57] Lebow and Stein, We all lost the Cold War, p. 97
[58] Lebow and Stein, We all lost the Cold War, p. 97

[59] ibid p. 140
[60] ibid p. 124
[61] McCauley, The Khrushchev era, Longman, , Harlow 1995, p.83
[62] Khrushchev, Khrushchev remembers, p.493
[63] Lebow and Stein, We all lost the Cold War, p. 94
[64] ibid p. 68
[65] Khrushchev, Khrushchev remembers, p. 494
[66] Lebow and Stein, We all lost the Cold War, p. 97
[67] ibid p. 110
[68] LaFeber, America, Russia and the Cold War, McGraw-Hill Higher Education, New York 2002, p 330
[69] Williamson D, Europe and the Cold War 1945-9, p. 170
[70] Sanders V, The USA and Vietnam 1945-75, Hodder &Stoughton, London 1998, p. 62
[71] Brown and Mooney, Cold War to Detente, Heineman Educational, Oxford1981, p. 138
[72] ibid p. 139
[73] Sanders V, The USA and Vietnam 1945-75, p. 62
[74] Ball, The Cold War, p. 150
[75] ibid p. 160
[76] ibid p. 178
[77] ibid p. 180
[78] ibid p. 185
[79] McCauley M, Russia, America &the Cold War, p. 62
[80] Ball, The Cold War, p. 176
[81] ibid p. 177
[82] ibid p. 185
[83] ibid p. 186
[84] Williamson D, Europe and the Cold War 1945-9, p. 171
[85] Ball, The Cold War, p. 190
[86] ibid p. 196
[87] ibid p. 212
[88] http://americanrhetoric.com/speeches/ronaldreaganevilempire.htm
[89] Hanimäki and Westad, The Cold War, p. 573-579
[90] Bell PMH, The Cold War since 1945, Arnold, London 2001, p. 357
[91] Hanimäki and Westad, The Cold War, p 587
[92] McCauley M, Russia, America &the Cold War, Second Edition, Pearon Education Ltd, Harlow 2004, p. 118
[93] Mc Williams and Piotrowski, The Cold War since 1945, Adamantine Press Ltd, London 1993, p. 455
[94] Bell PMH, The Cold War since 1945, p. 367
[95] McCauley M, Russia, America &the Cold War, p. 93
[96] Gaddis JL., The Cold War, The Penguin Press, Ney York 2005, p. 245
[97] McCauley M, Russia, America &the Cold War, p. 118
[98] LaFeber, America, Russia and the Cold War, p 332
[99] Gaddis JL., The Cold War, p. 213
[100] Crockatt R, The Fifty Years War, p. 311
[101] McCauley M, Russia, America &the Cold War, p. 62
[102] Crockatt R, The Fifty Years War, p.362
[103] Ball, The Cold War, p. 243
[104] Gaddis JL., The Cold War, p. 193
[105] Gorbachev M, Michael Gorbachev Memoirs, Doubleday, New York 1995, p. xxvii
[106] LaFeber, America, Russia and the Cold War, p. 307
[107] Crockatt R, The Fifty Years War, p. 360
[108] Gaddis J L, The United States and the end of the Cold War, Oxford University Press, New York 1992, p. 161
[109] McCauley, Russia, America and the Cold War, p. 115
[110] Crockatt R, The Fifty Years War, p. 344
[111] LaFeber, America, Russia and the Cold War, p. 335
[112] Crockatt R, The Fifty Years War, p. 350
[113] ibid p. 350
[114] Gaddis., The Cold War, p. 245
[115] Crockatt R, The Fifty Years War, p. 346
[116] Bell P M H, The Cold War since 1945, p. 382
[117] Gorbachev M, Michael Gorbachev Memoirs, p. xxvii

[118] ibid p. 674
[119] Bell P M H, The Cold War since 1945, p. 357
[120] ibid p. 376
[121] ibid p. 388
[122] ibid p. 387
[123] New York Times October 28, 1992
[124] New York Times November 6, 1992
[125] Crockatt R, The Fifty Years War, p. 341
[126] ibid p. 341
[127] McCauley, Russia, America and the Cold War, p. 4
[128] Bell, The Cold War since 1945, p. 388
[129] Gaddis J L, The United States and the end of the Cold War, p. 166